A COUNTRY
CROSS-STITCH
COMPANION

A COUNTRY
CROSS-STITCH
COMPANION

Lynda Burgess

Photographs by Amanda Heywood

SMITHMARK

This edition published in 1997 by
Smithmark Publishers, a division of U.S. Media Holdings Inc.
16 East 32nd Street, New York, NY 10016.

SMITHMARK books are available for bulk purchase for sales promotion and for
premium use. For details write or call the Manager of Special Sales, SMITHMARK
Publishers, 16 East 32nd Street, New York, NY 10016; (212) 532-6600.

ISBN 0-7651-9577-1

Produced by Anness Publishing Limited
Hermes House
88-89 Blackfriars Road
London SE1 8HA

Previously published as three separate volumes, *Step-by-Step 50 Nature Cross-Stitch
Designs*, *Step-by-Step 50 Country Garden Cross-Stitch Designs* and *Step-by-Step 50
Victorian Needlecraft Designs*

Printed and bound in Hong Kong

1 3 5 7 9 10 8 6 4 2

CONTENTS

INTRODUCTION

Everyone yearns to be creative, but not everyone is confident that they have the necessary skills and ability. Cross stitch is a great pastime because it gives people who long to create the opportunity to be artistic – even if they don't feel they have a wealth of artistic talent. If you can master the simple cross stitch and follow a chart, you can make beautiful pictures that will last a lifetime and become heirlooms for future generations. It couldn't be easier. This book is a library of designs with the ever-popular country theme and has a wealth of nature and wildlife designs for cross stitchers of all levels of ability. Whether you're just a beginner or a more accomplished and experienced stitcher, you're sure to find something you'll want to stitch.

And if as a beginner you want to try one of the more complicated projects, don't worry, the step-by-step instructions will take you through any stitch or method that may seem a little difficult.

Before you start stitching, there are a couple of things to consider. To ensure perfect pictures every time, make sure that all the stitches run in the same direction. Do not pull the stitches too tight. When working stitches to the left, pull the needle towards your left shoulder and when working stitches to the right, pull towards the right. Many stitchers find that hours of continuous stitching cause their shoulders to start aching. To avoid this, work with a lamp behind your stitching shoulder – the heat from the light keeps the muscles warm – and be sure to stretch your shoulder muscles every half-hour.

All projects are worked in Anchor threads, although colour descriptions are given in each key so that you can work with your own threads and match the colours. In some projects, a sewing machine has been used, although every design that calls for a machine can also be made up by hand.

There's a wealth of design ideas to keep nature lovers occupied. As you leaf through the pages and decide on your first project, you're just beginning hours of enjoyable and creative cross stitching.

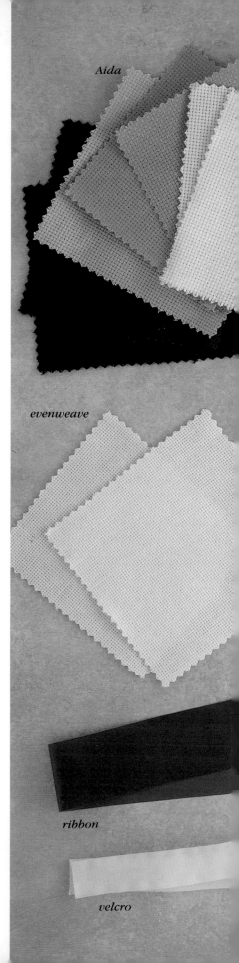

Aida

evenweave

ribbon

velcro

Materials

A variety of materials are used in this book, all of which should be available from your local craft stockist, but if not, try one of the suppliers listed at the back of the book.

Aida
This is the most popular fabric for cross stitch. It is a cotton fabric available in a variety of colours. There are holes between the warp (vertical) and weft (horizontal) threads into which you make your cross stitches. Fabric sizes are designated by the number of holes per inch, for example, 14 holes per inch (hpi) will give you 14 stitches every inch of fabric. The most common counts of Aida in the shops are 11, 14, 16, 18 and 22. The easiest to work on is probably 14 hpi as the holes are easy to see and your work grows fairly quickly.

Aida plus
This is a relatively new, sturdy fabric with a paper-like quality, ideal for bookmarks and projects that require moulding, folding and cutting. Available in 14 hpi.

Aida band
This is ideal for making a cross-stitch border to add to a towel or curtain. It is available in widths from 2.5 to 10 cm (1 to 4 in) and a range of colours.

Aida tea towel
This is a standard kitchen tea towel with an Aida band woven across one edge, creating an original and practical towel.

Evenweave
As the name suggests, the warp and the weft threads of this fabric are equidistant, forming small squares or blocks of holes around the threads. The stitches are worked into the holes, either across a single thread or, more commonly in cross stitch, two threads. Many of the projects in this book are worked over two threads on a 28 hpi evenweave.

Felt
This bonded fabric is ideal for backing your work as it does not fray. It is generally available in 18 cm (7 in) squares and in a wide range of colours.

Waste canvas
This is used for stitching a design on to a ready-made garment. Tack (baste) the canvas on to the garment, then stitch the design through both canvas and fabric. After completion, dampen slightly; the starch in the waste canvas dissolves and you can remove the threads.

Stranded cottons
The most common threads used for cross stitch are stranded cottons or embroidery floss. Each skein is made up of six stranded threads which can be separated. Most of the projects described in this book are worked in two strands.

Marlitt threads
These have a lustre and give your work an attractive, silky appearance, ideal for enhancing a motif design.

Kreinik blending filaments
Formerly known as Balger, Kreinik threads are sold as single strands on a card or bobbin. The threads look luxurious, with metallic blends of gold, silver, red, green and blue – ideal for adding dramatic detail.

Metallic threads
These are coarser than blending filaments and come in a variety of thicknesses. Although they can be used for cross stitch, they do not blend very well with the embroidery threads (floss).

Sewing threads
The sewing threads in the book are polyester threads. They are strong and work well on all sewing machines.

Beads
Work the first part of a half cross stitch and thread the bead on to the needle before inserting it back into the fabric to complete the half cross stitch. Beads are available from most craft shops in a variety of lustrous colours. You may prefer using a beading needle, which has a small head and a long, thin needle point.

Interfacing
This is a bonded fabric used to give support and stiffness, and to help to prevent distortion. It is available in sew-in or iron-on forms in a range of weights.

Wadding (Batting)
This is used to lift work when mounting it in cards, pots and frames. Wadding placed behind your work will keep the stitches plush and show them to their best advantage. It comes in a variety of weights; for cross stitch we recommend you use a 50 g (2 oz) wadding.

wadding
(batting)

fabric

beads

backing
and lining
fabric

piping cord

sewing
thread

stranded
cotton

interfacing

metallic
thread

thread

felt

cotton tape

Aida

metallic
thread

ribbon

zip (zipper)

Aida bands

Equipment

None of the equipment needed for cross stitch is bulky or heavy. Its portability is one reason why cross stitch is such a great hobby. You can do it anywhere. Once you have these few essential items to hand, you'll be ready to cross stitch.

All-purpose scissors
A sharp pair of all-purpose scissors is a good investment. Be sure to keep them for cutting fabric only, as anything else will dull the blades. A 13 cm (5 in) blade is excellent for most things. It is a good idea to buy a second, less expensive pair for slightly tougher tasks of cutting card, threads and tape, and in this way you will extend the life of both pairs.

Embroidery scissors
Embroidery scissors differ from ordinary, all-purpose scissors because the blades have sharp pointed tips, which enable you to cut behind stitches without cutting into the fabric. They are small and fit neatly into a handbag or work bag.

Snips
The primary purpose of these tiny clippers is snipping any stray threads. They are made of two facing blades, which are held together by a piece of strong wire. Like embroidery scissors, they fit neatly into a handbag or work bag.

Pins
Make sure you always use stainless steel pins because they do not rust. Rust marks on your work can be difficult to remove. Extra-fine long pins are the best, because they will not make lasting holes when pinning your work together. There are a variety of pins available, from gold-plated ones, which do not mark light-coloured fabric, to glass-headed pins which are easy to find.

Tapestry needles
Tapestry needles have a blunt end and a large eye. They come in a range of sizes. The most commonly used are 22, 24 and 26. The higher the number, the finer the needle. When working with a higher count fabric, it is advisable to use a finer needle. Most of the projects in the book call for a size 26.

Sharp needles
These needles, used for hand sewing, are long and have a fine sharp end. A longer needle is easy to manipulate in and out of the fabric and, being fine, it will not leave unsightly holes or marks in the fabric.

Tape measure
You can buy tape measures with both metric and imperial measurements. A plastic-coated measure is better than a cloth one, because with constant use the cloth tends to stretch out of shape so its measurements are not always as accurate as they should be. Use your tape measure for checking seam allowances and sizes of fabric.

Ruler
It you want a good ruler to use for your cross-stitch project, consider using a stainless steel one. A great advantage of a metal ruler is that it has a straight edge without any pitting. When you are cutting a straight edge of card or through layers of fabric, it is important that your ruler has a smooth edge. You can buy rulers with both metric and imperial measurements.

Double-sided tape
Double-sided tape is an absolute joy to have when making up cross-stitch projects. It is clean and wonderfully easy to use. You simply fix one side to your work, pull away the backing tape and join your surfaces together. It is especially good to use for putting together cards.

Pencil
You may need a pencil to mark out your projects. There are several different types of pencil you could choose. A fabric marker will disappear when you wash your fabric. For the projects in this book we have used a soft drawing pencil, worked lightly over the fabric. If you use it lightly it will leave only a faint mark which will not show on your finished work. However, if any marks can be seen, they are easy to wash off.

Tailor's chalk
Tailor's chalk is used for marking fabric. It comes in a variety of pale colours. You use the chalk to draw around templates and it leaves a light mark on the fabric. You should be able to brush the chalk away quite easily with a soft brush when you've finished working.

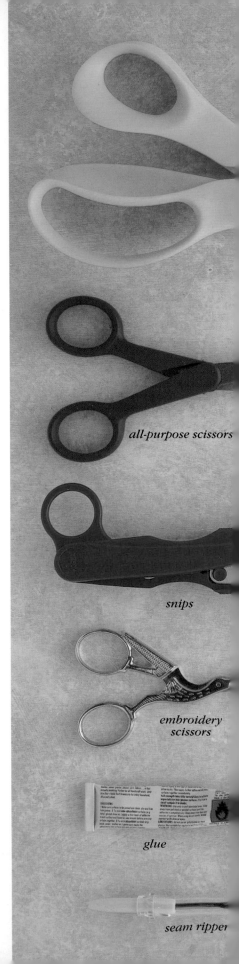

all-purpose scissors

snips

embroidery scissors

glue

seam ripper

pinking shears

double-sided tape

buttons

tape measure

tapestry needles

pins

sharp needles

tailor's chalk

embroidery frame

crochet hook

fabric marker

pencil

ruler

MADE IN ENGLAND

flexi-hoop

thimble

curtain rings

pins

TECHNIQUES

Cross stitch

If you want to become a cross-stitch expert, you should first master this simple stitch. It is the basic stitch from which all cross-stitch pictures are made.

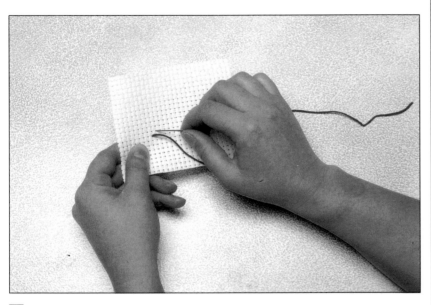

1 To make a cross stitch, first bring your needle up through the fabric in the bottom left-hand corner where you want the stitch to begin. Drop the needle back through the fabric in the top right-hand corner to make a diagonal stitch.

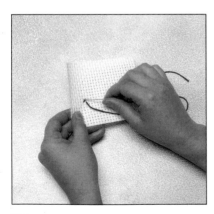

2 Bring the needle up through the fabric at the bottom right and drop it back through at the top left to complete the cross stitch.

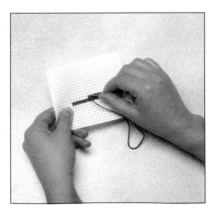

3 Repeat these steps to make a row of stitches.

Continuous cross stitch

If you're working large areas in a single colour, this method of creating cross stitches will save you both time and unnecessary effort.

 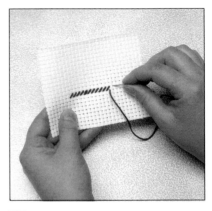

1 To make a cross stitch, take your needle up through the fabric in the bottom left-hand corner where you want the stitch to be. Drop the needle back through the fabric in the top right-hand corner to make a diagonal stitch.

2 Bring the needle up at the bottom right-hand corner of the first stitch and, moving towards the right, drop it back through the fabric in the following top right-hand corner. Repeat this step to form a row of half cross stitches.

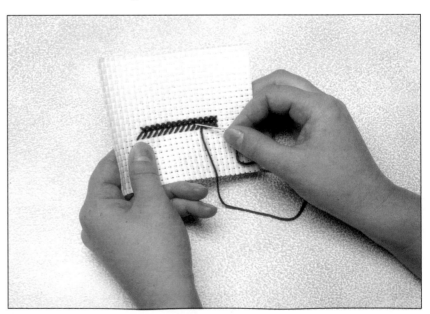

3 Turn the needle around, bringing it up through the fabric in the bottom right-hand corner and dropping it down at the top left. Repeat this step to finish off your crosses.

Half cross stitch

Sometimes a design may use a half cross stitch instead of a full one. Make one simply by working half a stitch. It is often used where the work requires a lighter touch.

1 First consider where you want to start stitching. Then, to make a half cross stitch, bring the needle through the fabric in the bottom left-hand corner of the stitch.

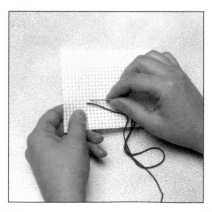

2 Moving towards the right, drop the needle back through the fabric in the following top right-hand corner to make a diagonal stitch.

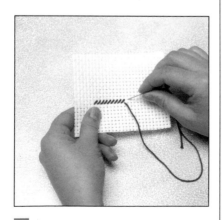

3 Repeat this step to form a row of half cross stitches.

Three-quarter stitch

When working a design, you may find that an area requires part of a stitch to be worked in one colour and the rest in a second colour. Look closely at your work to judge where the three-quarter stitch and the quarter stitch should lie.

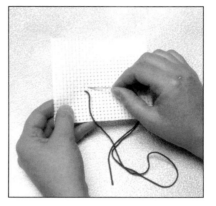

1 Bring the needle up through the fabric in the bottom left-hand corner of the stitch. Drop the needle back through the fabric in the top right-hand corner to make a diagonal stitch.

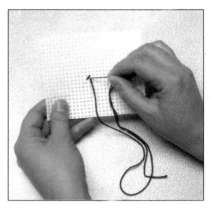

2 Bring the needle back through the fabric at the bottom right and drop it back halfway, directly in the middle of the stitch.

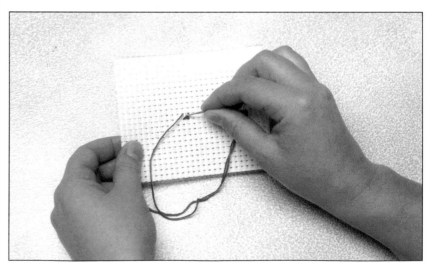

3 Change to a second colour of thread and bring the needle up through the fabric at the top left of the stitch. Drop it back through the fabric to meet the first colour in the middle of the stitch. This will complete your three-quarter stitch.

Long stitch

Long stitch can be used to add detail to your work. Although it is not used in all projects, it is a useful stitch to master should you wish to add some of your own definition.

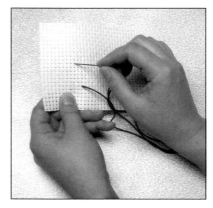

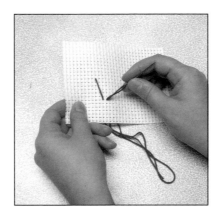

1 Bring the needle up through the fabric where you want the long stitch to begin.

2 Taking your needle across the fabric, drop it back through where you want the stitch to end. Pull the thread firmly but not too tightly.

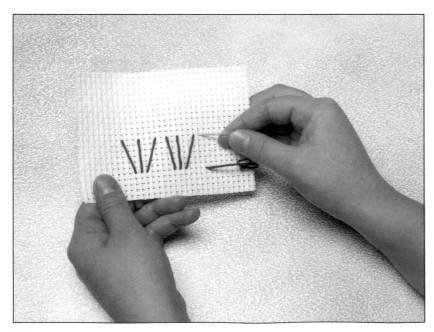

3 Repeat these steps, bringing the needle up through the fabric where you want the next stitch to start.

Backstitch

Used for outlining, backstitch is an essential stitch to master. By following the instructions below, you'll be an expert in minutes.

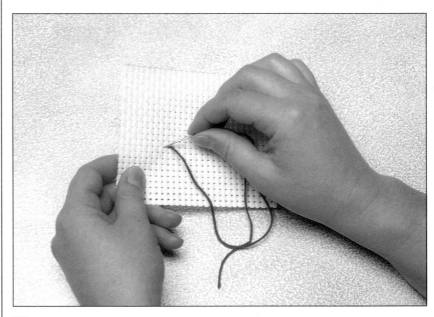

1 Bring the needle up through the fabric one hole ahead of where you want the stitch to begin. Drop the needle into the previous hole, bringing it up again one hole ahead of your original stitch.

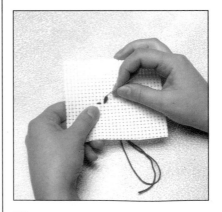

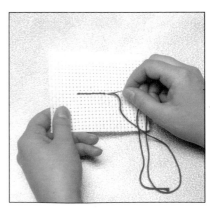

2 Drop the needle back through the fabric into the previous stitch and bring it up one hole ahead.

3 Repeat these steps to complete a row of backstitch.

French knot

French knots are created by wrapping the thread around the needle and pulling the needle back through the fabric. The textured knots are ideal for flower centres and for the middle of an animal's eye.

1 Bring the needle up through the fabric where you want the stitch to begin, then make a small stitch in the fabric but do not pull the needle out of the fabric.

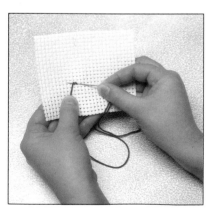

2 Wrap the thread twice around the needle and pull the needle through the loops, ensuring the loops work towards the end of the thread close to the fabric.

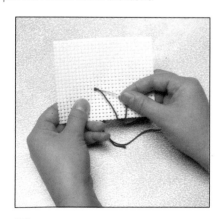

3 Drop the needle back through the fabric close to the knot and finish off on the underside.

Holbein stitch

Holbein stitch is an alternative to backstitch used for outlining your work. It is worked by making a running stitch, turning your work and filling the gaps as you work back to the starting point.

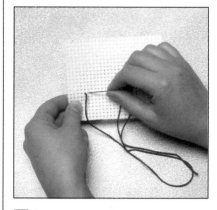

1 Bring the needle up through the fabric where you want the stitch to begin and drop it into the next hole to the right.

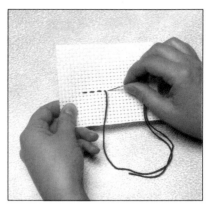

2 Continue in a running stitch, bringing the needle up and down into every other hole.

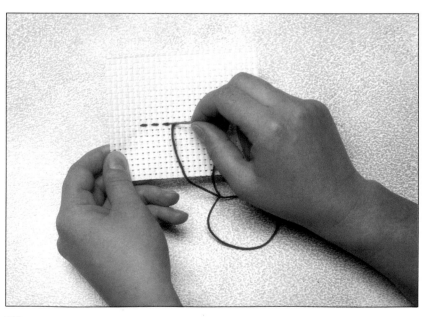

3 When you have worked a running stitch outline, turn the work around and sew a running stitch in the other direction, to fill the alternate gaps.

Lacing a picture

When you've finished stitching, you may decide to mount your work in a frame. You could send it to a framer but, by following the simple steps detailed below, you can prepare the picture for framing yourself.

1 Cut a piece of cardboard and a piece of wadding (batting) the same size as you want the finished framed work to be. With the design facing down, centre the wadding and then the card on the back of the work.

2 Fold over the top and bottom edges of the work, pinning them along the grain of the fabric to the top and bottom of the cardboard.

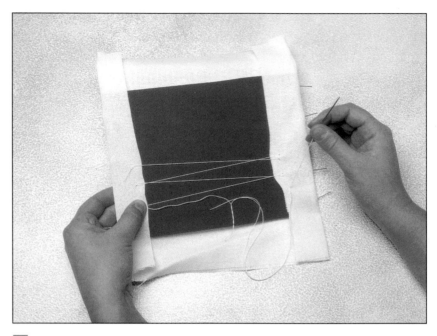

3 Starting from the centre, use lacing thread to work a herringbone stitch from side to side towards the bottom edge. Pull the sides tightly together. Repeat this step, working from the centre to the top edge.

4 Fold over the long edges, mitring the corners to keep them neat.

5 Repeat the lacing process on the long edges.

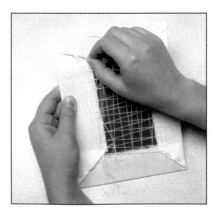

6 Finish the work by slip stitching the corners, and place it in a picture frame.

Filling a pot

Several of the projects in this book have been mounted in craft pots. This is a popular and easy mount for cross-stitch projects and pots are widely available in all good craft shops.

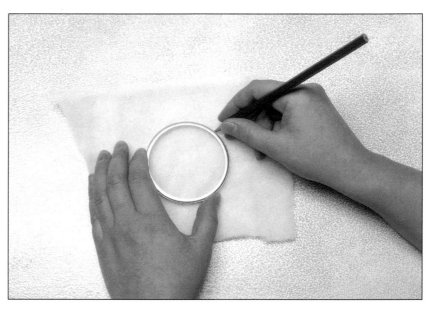

1 With the stitching face down, centre the lid over it and use a pencil to draw around it on the back of the work.

2 Cut around the pencil line. This will leave you with a design that will fit inside your pot.

3 Draw around the lid of the pot on to a piece of wadding (batting).

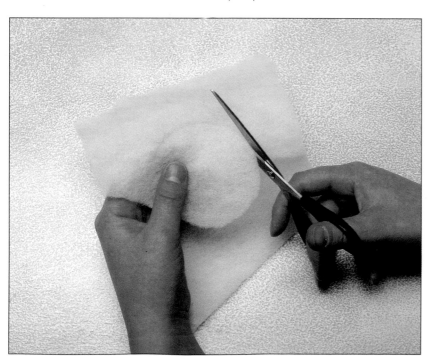

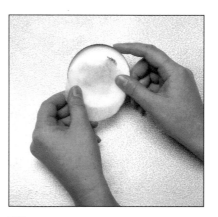

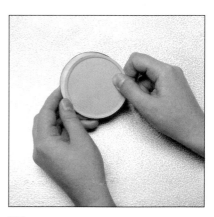

4 Cut out the circle from the wadding (batting).

5 Position the design inside the rim, with the embroidery facing into the lid. Place the wadding (batting) on top.

6 Fix the metal disk over both the design and the wadding (batting) to hold them firmly in place.

Filling a card

Once you have learned how to put your work into a card, you'll never be at a loss for a cross-stitch mount and your friends will love their personalized greetings.

1 Use a pencil to draw around the card opening on to the wadding (batting).

2 Cut around the pencil line.

3 Trim the edges of the design to make it slightly smaller than the front of the card.

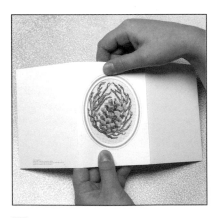

4 Place the design behind the middle section of the card so that the stitching is in the centre of the opening.

5 Place the wadding (batting) on the back of the design.

6 Stick double-sided tape around the edges of the middle section. Remove the backing and gently fold over the card edge to seal the design within the card.

Making a bookmark

Projects with a visible back and front need a properly finished back. A bookmark is a prime example of a project which needs this treatment. Use these easy step-by-step instructions to discover how you can give your work a truly professional finish.

1 Measure a piece of felt slightly smaller than the size of your bookmark.

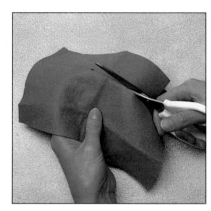

2 Cut the felt to size, taking care that the finished piece comes just inside the edges of the bookmark.

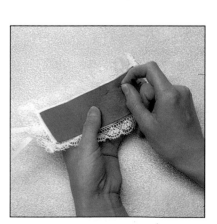

3 Pin the felt to the back of your work.

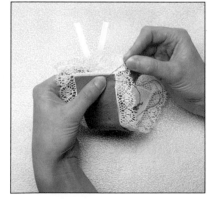

4 Using a small stitch, oversew (slip stitch) the felt, taking care the stitches don't show on the right side.

USING THE CHARTS

Each symbol on the chart represents one stitch. The key tells you how many strands of each colour to use for each area. Parts of the design may be outlined in backstitch, this is identified by lines around or through the symbols. We have given Anchor thread numbers throughout. In addition, we have also given colour descriptions, since you may wish to use other brands and manufacturer's threads are not exact equivalents. Finally, the stitch count gives you the finished size of your design: the first number is the height and the second the width.

Making a sachet or cushion

The Victorians loved keepsakes – small pillows, sachets, and pincushions. Gathered ribbon, lace or piping would be used to decorate the edges and they all required an opening to put the pad or stuffing inside. There are different ways to make the opening; two are illustrated here. This simple method is suitable for pincushions and sachets.

1 Cut two pieces of the fabric to the required size. Gather the ribbon or lace and tack (baste) along the seamline. Sew along the top edge.

2 With the right sides together, sew along the seamline leaving the top edge open. Trim the seams and corners before turning through. Insert the pad or stuffing and slip stitch the top edges.

This second method is more appropriate for cushion covers. To remove the pad easily, you can make an opening on the underside.

1 Cut two pieces of fabric each 8 cm (3¼ in) longer than the finished cushion. Make a 3 cm (1¼ in) hem along each of the short edges. Cut the two hemmed pieces of one piece of fabric apart in the centre. Overlap the hems and tack (baste) together. With the right sides together sew along all four edges. Trim the seams and corners before removing the tacking (basting) thread and turning through. Sew press studs (snap closures) along the opening if required.

Beadwork

Beads were very popular in Victorian times. They were originally sewn on canvas and used to decorate furniture, but later they were used to decorate purses, clothes, and jewellery. After the death of Prince Albert, black beads became fashionable as a sign of respect for the Queen. Beadwork is always worked with double thread and, in contrast to other forms of embroidery, begins with a secure knot.

 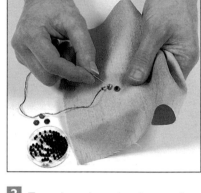

1 To stitch individual beads, work in running stitch or back stitch. Make the stitch the same length as the bead to prevent it fraying the thread.

2 To anchor a larger bead or sequin together, bring the thread through the sequin first, then thread on to the bead and sew back through the sequin again.

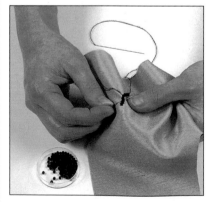

3 When sewing lots of beads it may be quicker to couch down a "string". Bring a bead needle through the fabric and thread on several beads. Using a separate needle and thread, couch (make an overcast stitch as close as possible to each bead) down the "string" in lines or randomly to fill an area.

Tassels

Victorian bookmarks, bags, and cushions were often finished with tassels. Some tassels are quite complex to make, but others may be produced quite simply. Mix threads, ribbons, and yarns to produce a variety of different effects.

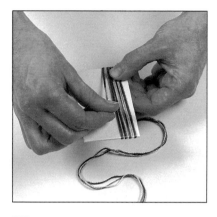

1 Wind threads round a piece of card (cardboard) 5 cm (2 in) wide and slightly deeper than the required length of tassel. Cut the threads along one edge and slide off the card (cardboard). Add a loop of ribbon or cord, stitch the ends securely and tuck beneath the threads.

2 Make a loop of thread and wrap the long end round the tassel till the band of threads is the required depth. Feed the end back through the loop and pull the other end gently till the loop is hidden beneath the wrapping and trim.

3 Alternatively, wrap a thread tightly round the tassel about 1 cm (½ in) from the loop end and tie a knot, leaving one long end. Using this thread, work a row of buttonhole stitches into the band. Continue round and round, working into the row below and making sure you do not stitch into the tassel itself. When you reach the top, thread the needle through all the loops, then pull it up tightly and finish off.

Bead tassel

More ornate tassels can be made from beads. These look similar to thread tassels but are made in a slightly different way.

1 Thread beads on to a strong thread until the string is the required length. Miss the last bead and take the needle and thread back through all the other beads. Make about 20 strings of beads and stitch securely at 7 mm (¼ in) intervals to a strip of felt 20 cm × 1 cm (8 in × ½ in).

2 Trim the end of the felt to a point. Sew a loop to the wide end, spread fabric glue along the centre, then roll up tightly. Stitch the end on to the felt and wrap with lurex yarn to create a neat rounded head. Cover with rows of beads on a double thread, stitching through the head to secure.

Fringe

Fringes were used to decorate the edges of scarves, cushions and bags. The threads were always attached in the same way each time, but some were knotted to create different effects.

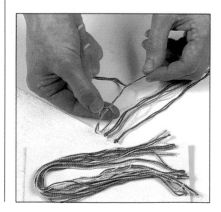

1 Sew double lengths of thread, slightly larger than actually required, through the hem with the loop on the right side. Feed the ends of the thread through the loop and pull tight. Repeat as often as necessary. Make a knotted fringe by tying bundles of threads together with an overhand knot.

Posy of pansies

Giving a card to someone you love reminds them how much you care. Make this floral posy as a special gift.

YOU WILL NEED
Design size: 36 x 47
fabric: 14 hpi Aida, 13 x 16 cm
  (4 ½ x 6¼ in)
26 tapestry needle
stranded cotton, as listed in key
wadding (batting)
card with opening
fabric-marker pen
scissors
double-sided tape

1 Work the cross stitch, beginning at the centre of the design. Use two strands of stranded cotton for all the cross stitch.

2 Once all the cross stitch is complete, use one strand of stranded cotton to create outlines in backstitch.

3 Neatly finish the work and mount it by following the instructions for filling a card.

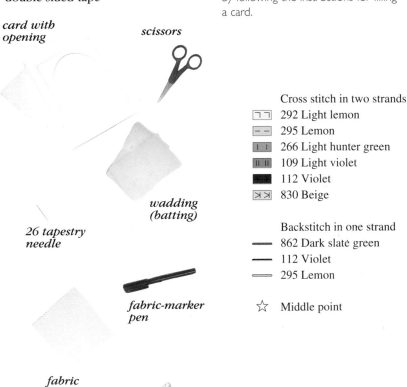

card with opening

scissors

wadding (batting)

26 tapestry needle

fabric-marker pen

fabric

stranded cotton

Cross stitch in two strands
⊓⊓	292 Light lemon
– –	295 Lemon
I I	266 Light hunter green
II II	109 Light violet
■■	112 Violet
⊠⊠	830 Beige

Backstitch in one strand
——	862 Dark slate green
—	112 Violet
═	295 Lemon

☆ Middle point

First snowdrops

Emerging through the new-fallen snow, the snowdrop peeks its delicate head, bringing with it a promise of new life and rich potential for the new year.

You will need
Design size: 22 x 34
fabric: 28 hpi over two threads,
  11 x 13 cm (4½ x 5 in)
26 tapestry needle
stranded cotton, as listed in key
oval craft pot
fabric-marker pen
scissors
wadding (batting)
tape measure

1 Work the cross stitch using two strands throughout.

2 Backstitch the detail marked on the chart using one strand throughout.

3 Neatly finish the work and mount by following the instructions for filling a pot.

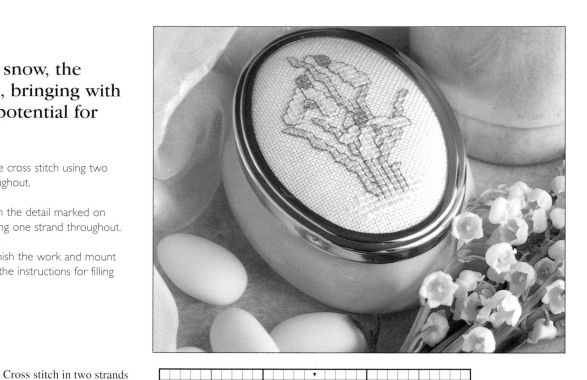

Cross stitch in two strands
- 255 Deep yellow green
- 253 Pale yellow green
- 275 Cream
- 1 White

Backstitch in one strand
— 281 Mid parrot green

☆ Middle point

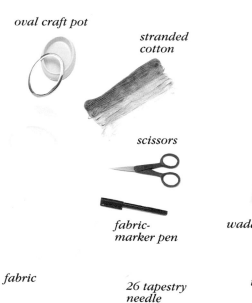

oval craft pot

stranded cotton

scissors

fabric-marker pen

fabric

26 tapestry needle

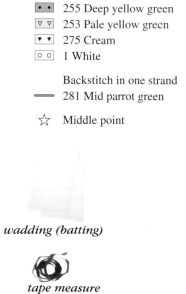

wadding (batting)

tape measure

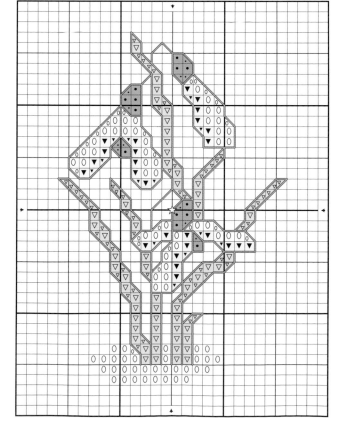

Spring cushion

Delicate blooms start to show after the harsh winter weather passes. Pushing through the soil, the first flowers of spring are a welcome reminder that the warmer weather is on its way.

YOU WILL NEED
Design size: 146 x 147
fabric: 14 hpi Aida, 36 x 36 cm
  (14 x 14 in)
26 tapestry needle
thimble
stranded cotton, as listed in key
backing fabric
tape measure
fabric-marker pen
scissors
pins
sharp needle
sewing thread
cushion pad
braid trim

backing fabric

tape measure

sewing thread

fabric-marker pen

scissors

thimble

needles

stranded cotton

pins

1 Work the cross stitch using two strands of stranded cotton.

2 Backstitch detail using one strand of stranded cotton on the flowers (*mid left*) in dark raspberry; on the leaf detail (*top right*) in dark forest green. Backstitch the detail on all the pink flowers using two strands of mid grey; on the stems (*top left*) using two strands of mid hunter green and on the flower details (*top right*) using two strands of deep rose. Stitch French knots in light blue randomly around the small blue flowers (*top left and bottom right*).

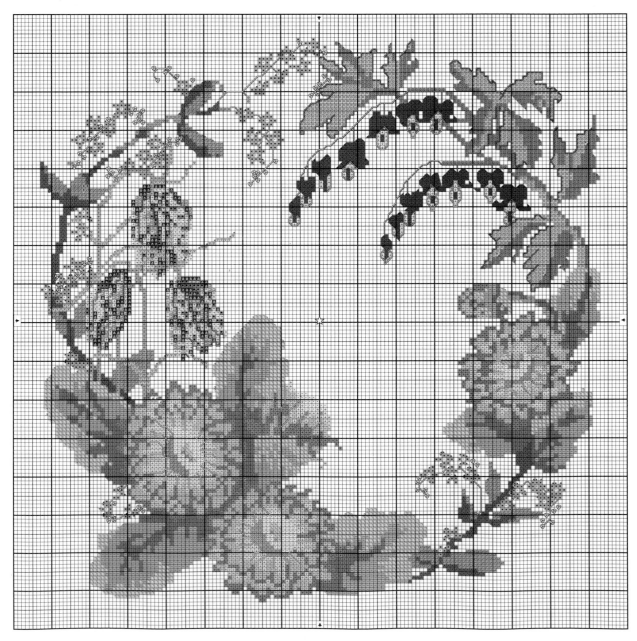

3 Neatly finish off the work before making into a cushion. To complete the cushion, cut four strips of contrasting fabric 8 cm (3 in) wide to border the cross stitch. Stitch the border around the design, sewing the shorter length to the sides first, and then the longer ones to the bottom. Cut a backing in the contrasting fabric the same size as the finished front piece. With right sides together, sew around the edges, leaving an opening to insert the cushion pad. Turn the design through to the right side. Insert the pad and slip stitch the opening shut. Add a braid trim.

Cross stitch in two strands

✶ ✶	129	Light blue
· ·	275	Cream
◣ ◣	297	Buttercup yellow
⊓ ⊓	254	Mid green
− −	256	Mid grass green
I I	268	Dark hunter green
+ +	55	Mid pink
÷ ÷	24	Rose pink
▲ ▲	277	Dark sage green
И И	853	Light sage green
↑ ↑	271	Light rose
⊐ ⊐	49	Light pink
■ ■	76	Deep rose
≡ ≡	78	Light raspberry
▲ ▲	70	Dark raspberry
→ →	276	Mid yellow
▽ ▽	293	Pale yellow
◇ ◇	306	Mid gold
← ←	255	Deep yellow green
↓ ↓	1026	Light dusky pink
▢ ▢	859	Bright leaf greeen
0 0	861	Leaf green

Backstitch in one strand

—	70	Dark raspberry
—	268	Dark forest green
—	399	Mid grey
—	267	Mid hunter green
—	76	Deep rose

French knots in two strands

᪲	129	Light blue
☆		Middle point

Violet glasses case

Dainty violets are an ideal motif for a practical spectacles case. Keep your glasses safe and clean in this attractive handbag-size case.

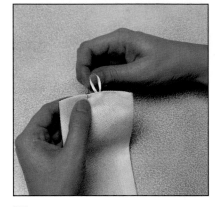

YOU WILL NEED

Design size: 23 x 27

fabric: 28 hpi evenweave over two threads, two pieces, 12 x 20 cm (4³/₄ x 8 in) and 12 x 28 cm (4³/₄ x 11 in)

26 tapestry needle

stranded cotton, as listed in key

tape measure

iron

interfacing

pins

sharp needle

sewing thread

lining fabric, two pieces, 11 x 28 cm (4¹/₄ x 11 in)

scissors

3 mm (¹/₈ in) satin ribbon

small button

stranded cotton

tape measure

sewing thread

sharp needle

fabric

26 tapestry needle

scissors

lining fabric

button

satin ribbon

interfacing

pins

MAKING-UP INSTRUCTIONS

1 First work the design on both pieces of fabric, using two strands for cross stitch and French knots, and one strand for backstitch. The bottom stitch of the motif should be approximately 4 cm (1¹/₂ in) from the lower edge of the smaller piece of fabric and approximately 3 cm (1¹/₄ in) from the lower edge of the larger piece. Iron interfacing to the back of both pieces of embroidery. With right sides facing, pin, then tack (baste) a piece of lining to the larger piece around three edges, then machine stitch.

2 Turn right side out. Fold a short piece of satin ribbon to make a loop and position it in the centre of the remaining short edge. Slip stitch this edge, enclosing the ribbon.

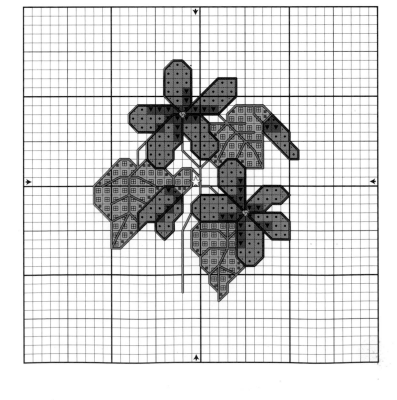

Cross stitch in two strands

97 Light violet

99 Mid violet

265 Very light hunter green

French knot in two strands

298 Orange

Backstitch in one strand

101 Dark violet

268 Dark hunter green

☆ Middle point

3 Repeat with the smaller piece of evenweave and lining, omitting the ribbon. Turn both pieces right side out and press.

4 Place the two pieces right sides together and stitch around the sides and lower edge, taking minimal turnings on sides. Stitch the button in place to close.

Apple-blossom coffee pot cover

Combine the evocative aromas of apple-blossom and coffee with this practical and charming coffee pot cover.

YOU WILL NEED
Design size: 147 x 91
fabric: 28 hpi evenweave over two
    threads, 30 x 20 cm (12 x 8 in)
26 tapestry needle
stranded cotton, as listed in key
iron
interfacing
2 pieces evenweave, 3 x 5 cm
    (1¼ x 2 in)
wadding (batting)
lining fabric
sharp needle
sewing thread
velcro
tape measure
pins
scissors

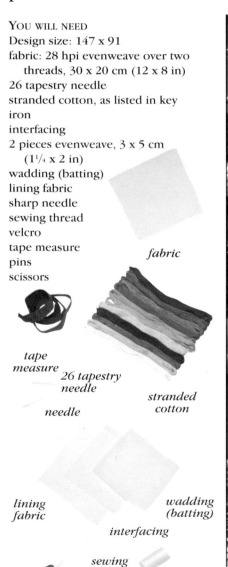

fabric

tape measure

26 tapestry needle

stranded cotton

needle

lining fabric

wadding (batting)

interfacing

sewing thread

scissors

pins

velcro

1 Work your design using two strands for cross stitch and one strand for all backstitch. Iron interfacing to reverse of piece. Fold two small pieces of evenweave in half lengthwise and stitch the two long edges to make the flaps. Turn right side out and press.

2 Place embroidered piece, wadding (batting) and lining, right sides together, enclosing small pieces of evenweave on each short side. Stitch around three sides, leaving the bottom open. Turn right side out and press.

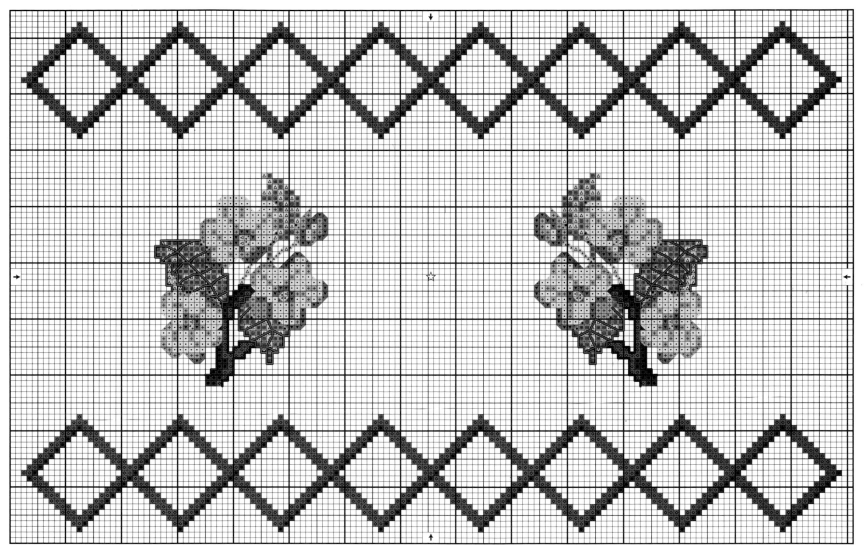

3 Sew one piece of velcro to each flap.

4 Stitch up remaining bottom edge.

Cross stitch in two strands

⊞ ⊞	242 Mid green
▼ ▼	26 Dark pink
◁ ◁	291 Yellow
● ●	370 Mid mink
· ·	271 Light pink
+ +	73 Pale pink
△ △	240 Light grass green
◇ ◇	369 Mid rust

Backstitch in one strand

——	879 Very dark forest green
——	78 Very dark pink
——	359 Dark brown

☆ Middle point´

Bird bookmark

You'll never lose your page again once you've made this decorative bookmark. The appearance of the blue tit (blue bird) tapping away at a milk bottle is a sure sign that spring is really here.

YOU WILL NEED
Design size: 28 x 98
fabric: bookmark, 18 hpi Aida
  8 x 18 cm (3 x 7 in)
26 tapestry needle
stranded cotton, as listed in key
felt
scissors
pins
sharp needle
sewing thread

bookmark

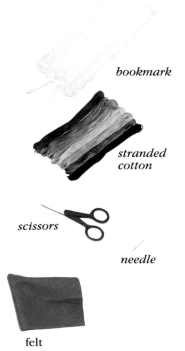

stranded cotton

scissors

needle

felt

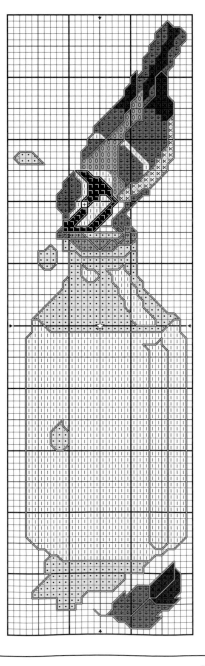

Cross stitch in one strand

• •	880 Flesh
⊓⊓	403 Black
I I	1 White
+ +	400 Slate grey
⊹⊹	398 Pearl grey
≑ ≑	433 Periwinkle blue
✕✕	149 Mid royal blue
⊠⊠	288 Pale yellow
0 0	186 Pale green

Backstitch in one strand

——	403 Black
——	400 Slate grey

☆   Middle point

1 Work the cross stitch using one strand throughout.

2 Add backstitch details in one strand for each colour.

3 Neatly finish the work by following the instructions for making a bookmark.

Bird in the bath

Spring brings with it the first birds out looking for food. Along with the first signs of colour and new growth, the birds symbolize the beginnings of a new season.

YOU WILL NEED

Design size: 29 x 59
fabric: 28 hpi evenweave over two
   threads, 10 x 10 cm (4 x 4 in)
26 tapestry needle
stranded cotton, as listed in key
oval frame
cardboard
fabric-marker pen
wadding (batting)
scissors
pins
sewing thread

oval frame

*stranded
cotton*

*wadding
(batting)*

fabric-marker pen   *scissors*

*26 tapestry
needle*

fabric

1 Work the cross stitch using two strands of stranded cotton for the bird, birdbath and grass. Use one strand for the remainder of the cross stitch.

2 Using one strand, backstitch around the birdbath. Backstitch the beak and legs of the black bird with two strands of dark lemon. Use two strands of dark lemon wrapped once around the needle for the eye. Use two strands of white wrapped twice around the needle for random French knots on the grass, to represent daisies.

3 Mount your work by following the instructions for lacing a frame.

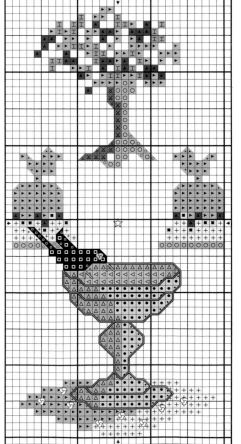

Cross stitch in two strands
for bird, bath and grass.
Use one strand for the rest.

△ △	399 Mid grey
▲ ▲	57 Dusky rose
I I	24 Rose pink
◄ ◄	167 Turquoise
► ►	266 Light hunter green
● ●	234 Light slate grey
○ ○	372 Mocha
✕ ✕	375 Beige
+ +	852 Dusky yellow
■ ■	297 Buttercup yellow
▢▢	403 Black

Backstitch in one strand
—— 889 Dark brown

Backstitch in two strands
═══ 290 Dark lemon

French knots in two strands
🌀 290 Dark lemon
🌀 1 White

☆ Middle point

Nightgown case

Keep your nightgown neat and clean in this fresh and elegant case. Simply stitch the design and with a little know-how turn it into a practical and attractive holdall.

1 Work the cross stitch in two strands throughout.

2 Backstitch the details in one strand throughout.

YOU WILL NEED
Design size: 122 x 114
fabric: 14 hpi Aida,
  23 x 29 cm (9 x 11½ in)
26 tapestry needle
stranded cotton, as listed
  in key
backing fabric
tape measure
fabric-marker pen
scissors
pins
sharp needle
sewing thread
wadding (batting)
3 snap fasteners

wadding (batting)

fabric

backing fabric

pins

scissors

sewing thread

stranded cotton

needles

tape measure

Cross stitch in
two strands

• •	288 Pale yellow
⊓ ⊓	289 Yellow
– –	291 Sunshine yellow
▮ ▮	263 Very deep olive green
‖ ‖	262 Olive green
+ +	260 Moss green
▪|▪ ▪|▪	267 Mid hunter green
⋮ ⋮	266 Light hunter green
✕ ✕	264 Yellow green
⋉ ⋉	1 White
∧ ∧	403 Black
✳ ✳	397 Light grey
⊟ ⊟	1041 Dark grey
● ●	175 Mauve
■ ■	176 Mid mauve
↖ ↖	177 Mauve blue
← ←	306 Mid gold
↓ ↓	288 Pale yellow
⊥ ⊥	289 Yellow
○ ○	291 Sunshine yellow
⋮⋮ ⋮⋮	214 Leaf green
▶ ▶	215 Light leaf green
◥ ◥	216 Light green
⋈ ⋈	875 Light blue green

Backstitch in
one strand

——	307 Gold
——	875 Ecru
——	273 Grey
——	274 Blue grey
☆	Middle point

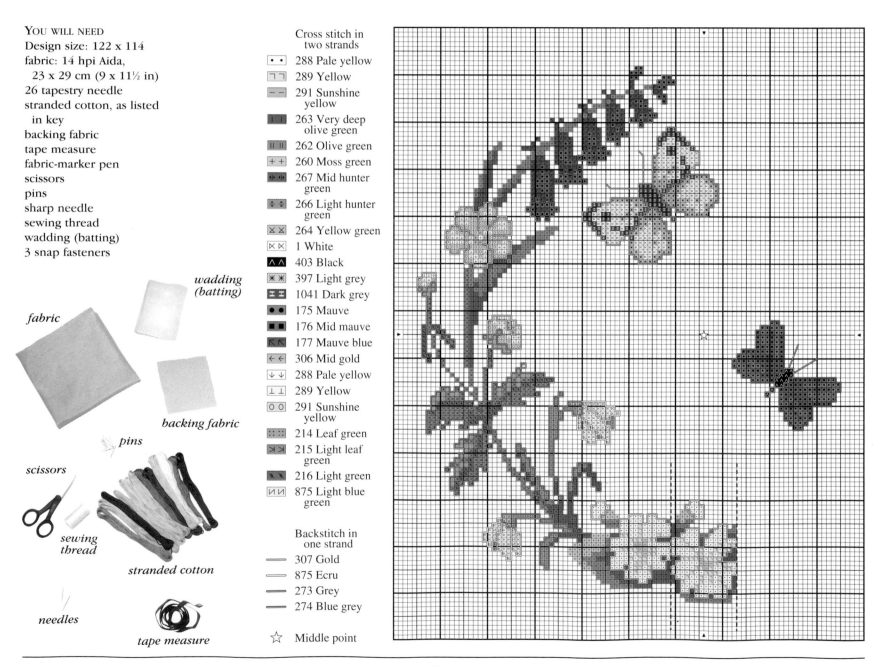

MAKING-UP INSTRUCTIONS

1 Leave a four-row border around the embroidery and attach 8 cm (3 in) wide strips of backing fabric, at least 8 cm (3 in) longer at each end than the embroidered panel. Mitre the corners by folding two adjacent edges together across the corner, right sides together. Stitch from the corner of the embroidery to the outside edge of the border at an angle of 45 degrees. Repeat for all four corners. Attach the wadding (batting) to the back of the work by tacking (basting) around the inside edge of the front panel.

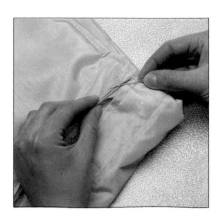

2 Cut backing to the same size as panel and edging strips. Tack (baste) the backing fabric, right sides together, to the embroidered panel, leaving a gap: you now have the embroidered layer, the wadding (batting) and the backing. Turn to the right side and press. Fold the top edge of the backing fabric under 1.5 cm (⅝ in) and press.

3 Turn under the top edge of front facing of bag 1.5 cm (⅝ in) and stitch in place. With right sides together, sew along the edges and bottom of the bag section. Turn to the right side and press. Tack (baste) the embroidered panel and the bag section right sides together, the back of the bag against the front of the embroidered panel, and stitch the raw edge at the top of the bag. Slip stitch the inside edge enclosing all the seams. Sew three snap fasteners at the lower edge of the flap.

Trout print

Moving slowly along the river, drifting through the gentle current, the smooth movement of the trout provides a tranquil respite from the hurried rush of everyday life.

YOU WILL NEED
Design size: 73 x 87
fabric: 28 hpi evenweave over two
    threads, 25 x 30 cm (10 x 12 in)
26 tapestry needle
stranded cotton, as listed in key
iron
towel
picture frame
ruler
pencil
cardboard
wadding (batting)
scissors
pins
sharp needle
sewing thread

Cross stitch in two strands

⊞ ⊞	168 Dark blue
S S	213 Very light leaf green
⊠ ⊠	215 Light leaf green
● ●	235 Mid grey
■ ■	236 Dark grey
↓ ↓	361 Light brown
✳ ✳	363 Dark brown
▽ ▽	858 Mint green
· ·	928 Light blue
∃ ∃	6 Light salmon
▼ ▼	9 Dark salmon
◇ ◇	234 Light grey

Backstitch in one strand
——   236 Dark grey

French knot in two strands
⊘   361 Light brown

☆   Middle point

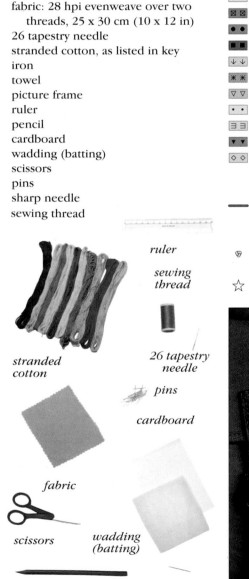

stranded
cotton

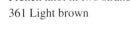
ruler

sewing
thread

26 tapestry
needle

pins

cardboard

fabric

scissors

wadding
(batting)

pencil

sharp needle

1 Work the design using two strands for cross stitch and one for backstitch.

2 When the work is complete, check it for marks. If it is grubby, you can rinse the stitching in warm, soapy water.

3 Allow it to dry flat and press lightly with the stitching face down on a towel so that you don't flatten the stitches.

4 Mount your work by following the instructions for lacing a picture.

Otter pot

Look for the otter basking at the river's edge; it is a sure sign that spring has returned.

YOU WILL NEED
Design size: 33 x 32
fabric: 18 hpi Aida,
    10 x 10 cm (4 x 4 in)
26 tapestry needle
stranded cotton, as listed in key
iron
towel
7 cm (2½ in) craft pot
pencil
scissors
wadding (batting)

1 Starting from the centre of the design, work the otter using one strand throughout.

2 When the work is complete, check it for marks. If it is grubby, you can rinse the stitching in warm, soapy water.

3 Allow it to dry flat and press lightly with the stitching face down on a towel so that you don't flatten the stitches.

4 Mount your work by following the instructions for filling a pot.

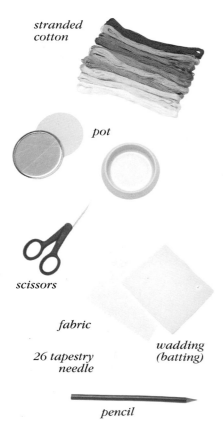

stranded cotton

pot

scissors

fabric

26 tapestry needle

wadding (batting)

pencil

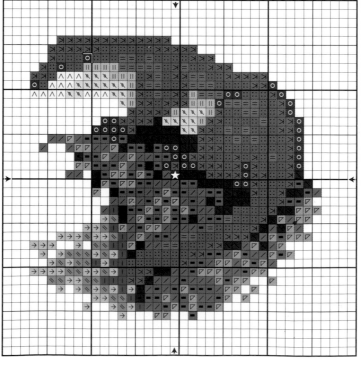

Cross stitch in one strand

⎮⎮	878 Dark forest green
■ ■	382 Very dark brown
◺ ◺	876 Mid forest green
→ →	875 Light forest green
▽ ▽	843 Dark green
╱ ╱	845 Sage
▬ ▬	681 Dark grey brown
◥ ◥	846 Brown
∧ ∧	926 Mid cream
▨ ▨	390 Deep cream
‖ ‖	391 Mushroom
═ ═	392 Dark mushroom
∴ ∴	903 Mid mushroom brown
▷◁	393 Very dark mushroom
○ ○	905 Mink brown

— Backstitch in one strand
391 mushroom

☆ Middle point

Duckling school gym bag

Pack your child off to school with a new and personal gym bag with their clean kit tucked inside. It's easy to make and any child will be proud to use it.

YOU WILL NEED
Design size: 117 x 120
fabric: 14 hpi Aida, 32 x 36 cm
  (13 x 14 in)
26 tapestry needle
stranded cotton, as listed in key
backing fabric
pins
sharp needle
sewing thread
scissors
tape measure
cord

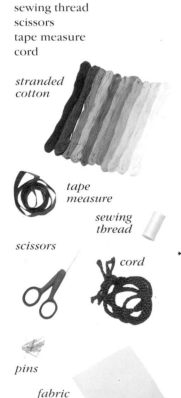

stranded cotton

tape measure

sewing thread

scissors

cord

pins

fabric

26 tapestry needle

sharp needle

MAKING-UP INSTRUCTIONS

1 First work the design using two strands for cross stitch and one strand for backstitch. With right sides facing, pin and tack (baste) the embroidered piece to the backing fabric along the bottom and side edges.

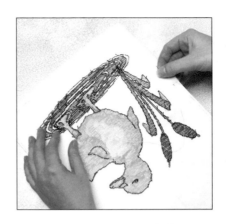

2 Sew along the bottom and the two long sides, leaving a 4 cm (1½ in) gap at the top of one long edge. Turn the top edge under 2 cm (¾ in) and stitch close to the raw edge. Turn the bag to the right side.

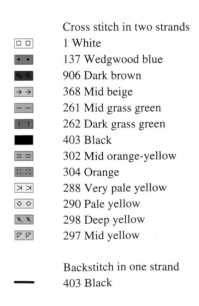

Cross stitch in two strands

□ □	1 White
• •	137 Wedgwood blue
■	906 Dark brown
→ →	368 Mid beige
– –	261 Mid grass green
I I	262 Dark grass green
■	403 Black
= =	302 Mid orange-yellow
⋮ ⋮	304 Orange
⤱ ⤱	288 Very pale yellow
◇ ◇	290 Pale yellow
↘ ↘	298 Deep yellow
▽ ▽	297 Mid yellow

Backstitch in one strand

— 403 Black

☆ Middle point

3 Thread the cord through the casing at the top of the bag. Finish by tying the ends of the cord in a knot.

TIP

When you spend a lot of time cross stitching you may find that your arm and shoulder feel stiff. Work with a light shining over your shoulder; the heat from the lamp will keep your muscles warm. Remember to stretch out your muscles every half-hour to keep them supple.

Alphabet sampler

This traditional design is characteristic of the alphabet samplers completed by young girls in the nineteenth century. Flowers, birds and butterflies were extremely popular motifs in Victorian times. Although quite large, the design is easily made following the simple cross-stitch chart.

Cross stitch in two strands

✕✕	143 Dark blue
■■	130 Pale blue
◆■	263 Dark green
⋁⋁	258 Light green
◉◉	39 Dark pink
⊞⊞	33 Light pink
⋈⋈	359 Brown
⊓⊓	307 Gold

Backstitch in one strand
— 359 Brown

☆ Middle point

TIP
Once the embroidery is complete it can be washed in mild soap suds if necessary. Rinse well and iron on the reverse side while still damp.

YOU WILL NEED
Design size: 130 x 120
fabric: 28 hpi evenweave,
　41 x 41 cm (16 x 16 in)
sharp needle
tacking (basting) thread
embroidery frame
26 tapestry needle
stranded cotton, as listed in key
cardboard
ruler
pencil
white cotton, 30 x 30 cm
　(12 x 12 in)
picture frame

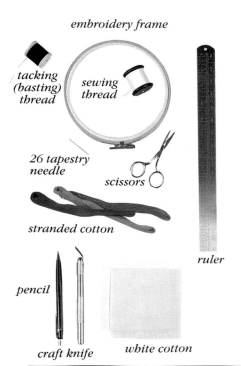

embroidery frame

tacking (basting) thread

sewing thread

26 tapestry needle

scissors

stranded cotton

ruler

pencil

craft knife　*white cotton*

1 Fold over a small turning on all edges of the evenweave and stitch down to prevent fraying. Fold the fabric in half in both directions and mark guide lines with thread. Place fabric in embroidery frame. Begin embroidering from the centre of the material. Work each stitch over two threads of linen. Use two strands of cotton for the cross stitch and a single strand for backstitch. Fasten the threads on and off rather than taking a colour across the back of the work.

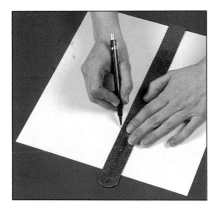

2 Cut a piece of cardboard 29 x 27 cm (11½ x 10½ in). Draw a line down the middle crossways. Measure 4.5 cm (1¾ in) down from the top and 5 cm (2 in) up from the bottom. Mark the middle point and draw a line lengthways.

3 On the sampler measure 4.5 cm (1¾ in) up from the top of the design and 4.5 cm (1¾ in) from the edge of the alphabet at each side. Mark the guide lines with tacking (basting) thread. Tack (baste) a further line 5 cm (2 in) down from the bottom. Back the work with the piece of white cotton and stretch over the cardboard using the guidemarks and tacking (basting) threads to keep the fabric straight. Remove tacking (basting) threads and mount in a frame of your choice.

Bluebells cushion

Brighten up your sofa with this unique cushion decorated with a repeat design of bluebells.

Cross stitch in two strands

268 Dark hunter green		118 Mid blue
267 Mid hunter green		109 Light blue
266 Light hunter green		117 Very light blue
265 Very light hunter green		297 Buttercup yellow
119 Very dark blue		
111 Dark blue	☆	Middle point

YOU WILL NEED
Design size: 142 x 142
fabric: 14 hpi Aida, 30 x 30 cm
(12 x 12 in)
26 tapestry needle
stranded cotton, as listed in key
backing fabric
tape measure
scissors
pins
sewing thread
sharp needle
30 cm (12 in) zip (zipper)
28 cm (11 in) cushion pad

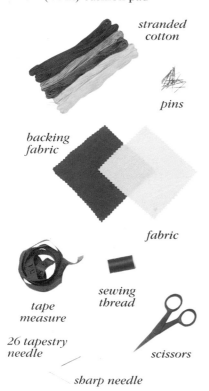

stranded cotton

pins

backing fabric

fabric

tape measure

sewing thread

26 tapestry needle

scissors

sharp needle

zip (zipper)

MAKING-UP INSTRUCTIONS

1 First work the design using two strands throughout. Lay the backing fabric over the embroidered piece with right sides facing. Stitch 1 cm (½ in) at either end of the top edge.

2 Insert the zip (zipper). With right sides facing, place the zip (zipper) behind the fabric. Tack (baste) and stitch the zip (zipper) to the edge of the backing fabric. Then tack (baste) and stitch the front piece to the zip (zipper).

3 Open the zip (zipper) slightly. With right sides facing, stitch around the three open sides. Clip the corners.

4 Unzip the cushion cover and turn it to the right side. Fill the cushion with the cushion pad.

Daisy shelf border

Repeat this reversed design to make a length of original shelf border. You could use it along kitchen or bedroom shelves or inside cupboards.

YOU WILL NEED
Design size: 22 x 128 repeat design
fabric: 14 hpi Aida band, 5 cm (2 in) wide band
26 tapestry needle
stranded cotton, as listed in key
sharp needle
sewing thread
scissors

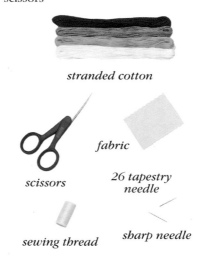

stranded cotton

scissors   *fabric*

26 tapestry needle

sewing thread   *sharp needle*

1 Working from the middle of the piece of Aida band, stitch the design in two strands for cross stitch and one strand for backstitch.

2 When you have worked one motif, start the next. The repeat motif begins 10 stitches into the previous one, so that the leaves overlap.

3 When you have finished the border, turn under each of the narrow edges and slip stitch in place.

Cross stitch in two strands
| | | 1 White
| • • | 298 Mid yellow
| ☐☐ | 227 Mid green

Backstitch in one strand
— 403 Black

☆ Middle point

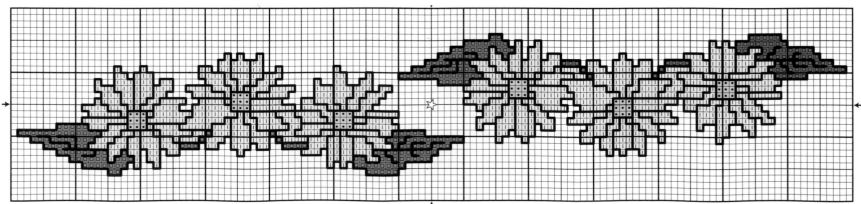

Swallows pot

Trinket boxes are always popular. This delicate swallow design is ideal for decorating a box to sit on your dressing-table.

YOU WILL NEED
Design size: 35 x 36
fabric: 18 hpi Aida, 10 x 10 cm
    (4 x 4 in)
26 tapestry needle
stranded cotton, as listed in key
iron
towel
7 cm (2½ in) craft pot
wadding (batting)
pencil
scissors

stranded cotton

pot

scissors

26 tapestry needle

wadding (batting)

pencil

fabric

1 Starting from the centre of the design, work the cross stitch using one strand throughout.

2 When the work is complete, check for marks. If it is grubby, you can rinse the stitching in warm, soapy water.

3 Allow it to dry flat and press lightly with the stitching face down on a towel so that you don't flatten the stitches.

4 Mount your work by following the instructions for filling a pot.

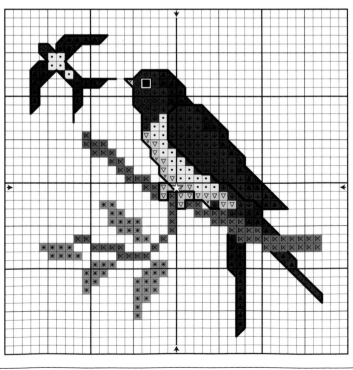

Cross stitch in one strand

▽ ▽	886 Dark cream
• •	926 Mid cream
✕ ✕	349 Brown
■	403 Black
◇ ◇	1006 Red
▲ ▲	150 Dark blue
✳ ✳	226 Green
↓ ↓	148 Blue

Backstitch in one strand

———	403 Black
═══	2 White
☆	Middle point

Primrose picture frame

If you are looking for an interesting frame, why not create your own with this attractive design?

YOU WILL NEED
Design size: 93 x 117
fabric: 28 hpi natural evenweave
    over two threads, 25 x 20 cm
    (10 x 8 in)
26 tapestry needle
stranded cotton, as listed in key
cardboard mount and backing
    board (pre-cut to size)
ruler
pencil
scissors
double-sided tape or glue
wadding (batting)
    (pre-cut to size)

stranded cotton

ruler

scissors

26 tapestry needle

cardboard mount

fabric

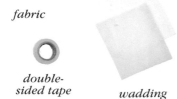

double-sided tape

wadding (batting)

pencil

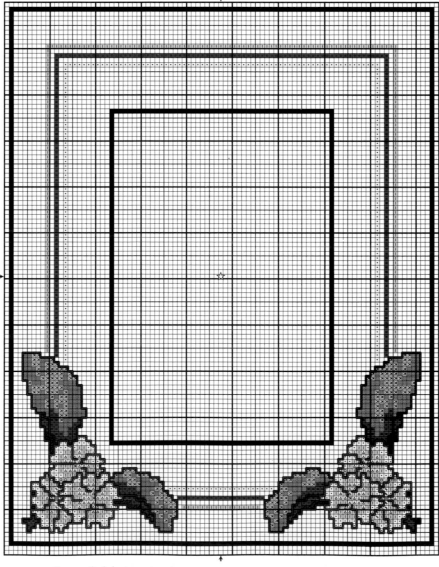

1 First stitch the design using two strands for cross stitch and one strand for backstitch. Place your pre-cut cardboard mount centrally over the design. Using a ruler and pencil, draw a cross from corner to corner of the aperture (opening).

2 Cut along the lines of the cross, taking care to cut into the corners. Cut out the middle section, leaving a 2 cm (³/₄ in) allowance. Position the pre-cut wadding (batting) and backing board on the back of the design.

Cross stitch in two strands

⌷⌷	298 Deep yellow
□□	297 Mid yellow
••	295 Pale yellow
◺◺	293 Yellow
△△	292 Cream

◢	269 Very dark hunter green
==	268 Dark hunter green
⠿	267 Mid hunter green
▷▷	265 Very light hunter green
■	403 Black

Backstitch in one strand

—	269 Very dark hunter green
—	905 Mink brown
☆	Middle point

3 Cut the edges of the fabric to within 2 cm (³/₄ in) of the mount board. Using double-sided tape, fold and stick the edges to the back of the board. Use double-sided tape to fix a piece of card to the back of the frame.

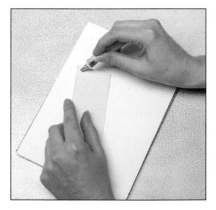

4 To finish, glue a cardboard stand to the back. If you prefer, you could use double-sided tape to fix the stand in place.

Spring cottage

The cottage garden offers rich pickings for flower lover and embroiderer alike. With pastel florals and colourful backgrounds, this cottage environment creates a perfect picture.

1 Work the cross stitch using two strands throughout.

2 Backstitch the details in one strand throughout.

3 Neatly finish off the work and mount it by following the instructions for lacing a frame.

YOU WILL NEED
Design size: 106 x 76
fabric: 30 hpi evenweave over
  two threads, 26 x 20 cm
  (10¼ x 8 in)
26 tapestry needle
stranded cotton, as listed in key
picture frame
cardboard
tape measure
fabric-marker pen
scissors
wadding (batting)
pins
sharp needle
sewing threads
frame

fabric

stranded cotton

scissors

fabric-marker pen

tape measure

26 tapestry needle

wadding (batting)

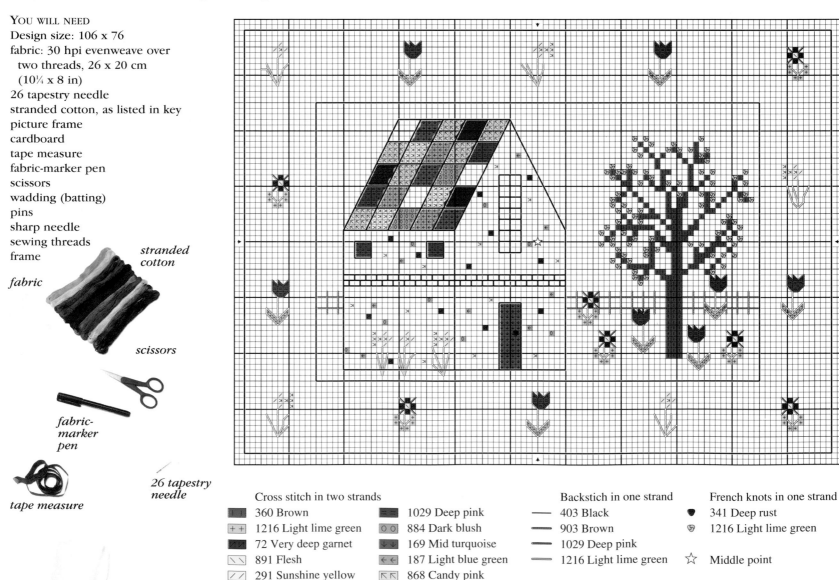

Cross stitch in two strands

ı ı	360 Brown	= =	1029 Deep pink
+ +	1216 Light lime green	o o	884 Dark blush
	72 Very deep garnet	↓ ↓	169 Mid turquoise
\ \	891 Flesh	← ←	187 Light blue green
/ /	291 Sunshine yellow	⊼ ⊼	868 Candy pink
⇥ ⇥	295 Lemon		

Backstich in one strand

— 403 Black
— 903 Brown
— 1029 Deep pink
═ 1216 Light lime green

French knots in one strand

♥ 341 Deep rust
🕸 1216 Light lime green

☆ Middle point

Blossom tree

Pale pinks and pastel greens bring the blossom tree to life. Delicate shades of emerging colour create a profusion of beauty unique to this time of year.

YOU WILL NEED
Design size: 28 x 28
fabric: 28 hpi evenweave over
  two threads, 10 x 10 cm
  (4 x 4 in)
26 tapestry needle
stranded cotton, as listed in key
crystal (glass) frame
scissors
fabric-marker pen

1 Work the cross stitch using two strands throughout.

2 Neatly complete the work. Cut the design to fit the frame using the opening of the frame as a guide for size. Mount in place.

crystal (glass)
frame

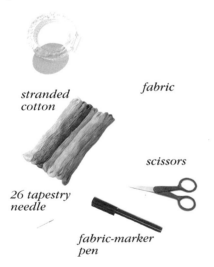

stranded
cotton

fabric

scissors

26 tapestry
needle

fabric-marker
pen

Cross stitch in two strands

✕✕	378 Light beige brown
●●	379 Mink brown
0 0	50 Deep pink
↖↖	271 Light rose
++	62 Dark pink
◁◁	259 Very light green
▶▶	265 Light green
☆	Middle point

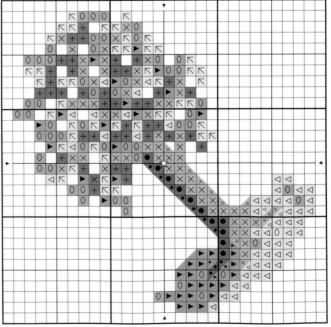

Baby fawn

With the spring comes the new – new plants, new flowers and new animals. The fragile fawn, newly born and finding its feet, evokes wonderful visions of the season to come.

YOU WILL NEED
Design size: 35 x 35
fabric: 28 hpi evenweave over
  two threads, 13 x 13 cm
  (5 x 5 in)
26 tapestry needle
stranded cotton, as listed in key
craft pot
fabric-marker pen
wadding (batting)
scissors

1 Work the cross stitch using two strands for the deer and also for the half cross stitch on the foreground scenery. Cross stitch the background foliage using one strand.

2 Backstitch the details marked on the chart using one strand throughout. Use one strand of white, twisted twice around the needle, for French knots for the eyes.

3 Neatly finish off the work and mount by following the instructions for filling a pot.

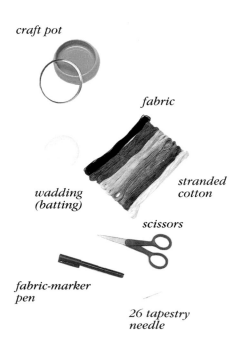

craft pot

fabric

wadding (batting)

stranded cotton

scissors

fabric-marker pen

26 tapestry needle

Cross stitch in two strands
▽ ▽	378	Light beige brown
Q Q	379	Mink brown
▬ ▬	376	Very light beige brown
▣ ▣	858	Mink green
⬤⬤	403	Black
∧ ∧	264	Yellow green
+ +	1	White

Backstitch in one strand
——	360	Brown
——	382	Very deep brown
——	243	Mid green
——	263	Very deep olive green

French knots in one strand
⊕	1	White

☆ Middle point

Love cushion

Finding the perfect token to express your love can often be difficult. This sentimental love cushion says it all.

1 Work the cross stitch using two strands throughout.

2 Backstitch the following details in one strand: the dove and flower outline, the eyes and the letters. Backstitch using two strands for the flower stems.

YOU WILL NEED
Design size: 73 x 77
fabric: 28 hpi evenweave over two
   threads, 20 x 22 cm (8 x 8½ in)
26 tapestry needle
stranded cotton, as listed in key
backing fabric
tape measure
scissors
pins
sharp needle
sewing thread
wadding (batting)
78 cm (31 in) length of 3 cm
   (1¼ in) white lace

Cross stitch in
   two strands

o o	307 Gold
• •	50 Deep pink
◊ ◊	62 Dark pink
⅂ ⅂	260 Moss green
I I	778 Pale pink
+ +	1 White
⋅⎮⋅ ⋅⎮⋅	933 Beige
÷ ÷	926 Off white
∧ ∧	167 Turquoise
и и	300 Light yellow
⋗ ⋗	210 Grass green
▲ ▲	236 Dark charcoal

Backstitch in
   one strand

——	8581 Dark grey
——	236 Dark charcoal
——	50 Deep pink
——	210 Grass green
——	260 Moss green
☆	Middle point

wadding (batting)

backing fabric

tape measure

sewing thread

lace

scissors

fabric

stranded cotton

pins

26 tapestry needle

MAKING-UP INSTRUCTIONS

1 Make a cushion pad: cut two 18 cm (7 in) squares of fabric. Stitch around three sides 5 mm (¼ in) from the edge. Turn to the right side, fill with wadding (batting). Slip stitch fourth side.

2 Stitch a running thread near the edge of the lace and gather up.

3 Sew lace to the right side of the backing fabric, leaving a 5 mm (¼ in) hem along each side and press on the wrong side. Slip stitch to the backing fabric. Where the lace and embroidery meet, sew another piece of lace 5 mm (¼ in) wide. Put both parts of the backing fabric right sides together and stitch along three sides 5 mm (¼ in) from the edge. Turn right sides out, insert the cushion pad, and sew up the remaining side.

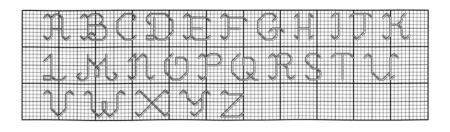

Spring sampler

A sampler provides a stitched record of a specific time. Remember a special time by marking the occasion with this original memento of the colours of spring.

YOU WILL NEED
Design size: 106 x 138
fabric: 28 hpi evenweave over
  two threads, 30 x 33 cm
  (12 x 13¼ in)
26 tapestry needle
stranded cotton, as listed in key
picture frame
cardboard
tape measure
fabric-marker pen
scissors
wadding (batting)
pins
sharp needle
sewing thread

1 Work the cross stitch using two strands throughout.

2 Work the backstitch detail, using one strand throughout.

3 Work the letters using two strands for cross stitch and one strand for backstitch.

4 Neatly finish the work. Mount the work by following the instructions for lacing a frame.

fabric

stranded cotton

wadding (batting)

needle

scissors

tape measure

fabric-marker pen

Cross stitch in two strands
⊓⊓ 40 Deep pink
↑↑ 403 Black
⌶⌶ 293 Pale yellow
△△ 295 Lemon
ʌʌ 260 Moss green
00 306 Mid gold
▽▽ 214 Leaf green
▨▨ 215 Light leaf green
◥◣ 176 Mid mauve
⋈⋈ 859 Bright leaf green
▽▽ 175 Light mauve
++ 861 Deep hunter green
●● 24 Rose pink
■■ 830 Beige
◤◥ 936 Dark brown
→→ 975 Pale blue
▬▬ 11 Coral red
△△ 48 Pale pink
↓↓ 216 Light green
╱╱ 264 Yellow green
◑◑ 267 Mid hunter green
✶✶ 266/267 Light hunter
      green/mid hunter green
‖‖ 888 Deep primrose yellow
⊥⊥ 292 Light lemon
-- 292/1 Light lemon/white
←← 307 Gold

Backstitch in one strand
— 401 Charcoal
— 40 Deep pink
— 306 Mid gold
— 307 Gold
— 176 Mid mauve
— 888 Deep primrose yellow
— 292 Cream
— 632 Dark brown

☆ Middle point

BUTTERFLY DETAIL

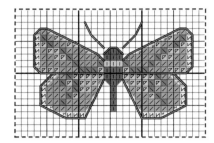

I Position the butterfly on the sampler.

Cross stitch in two strands
	400 Slate grey
	175 Light mauve
	175/1 Mauve/white
	176 Mid mauve
	176/1 Mid mauve/white

Backstich in one strand
— 401 Charcoal

☆ Middle point

Kingfisher shopping bag

Make yourself a colourful shopping bag covered in iridescent kingfishers. They sit in anticipation on a branch, waiting for food.

YOU WILL NEED
Design size: 158 x 66
fabric: 14 hpi Aida,
    46 x 15 cm (18 x 6 in)
26 tapestry needle
stranded cotton, as listed in key
Kreinik blending filaments, as listed
    in key
scissors
canvas fabric
calico lining fabric
tape measure
sharp needle
sewing thread
pins
iron

Kreinik blending filaments

sewing thread

pins

stranded cotton

tape measure

scissors

sharp needle

26 tapestry needle

canvas fabric

fabric

calico lining

MAKING-UP INSTRUCTIONS

1 First work the design using two strands throughout..Cut two 46 x 41 cm (18 x 16 in) pieces of the canvas fabric and the calico lining for the bag. Cut two 10 x 43 cm (4 x 17 in) strips of canvas fabric for handles. Turn under the long edges of the embroidered fabric by 1 cm (½ in). Tack (baste) and stitch on to the front piece of the bag.

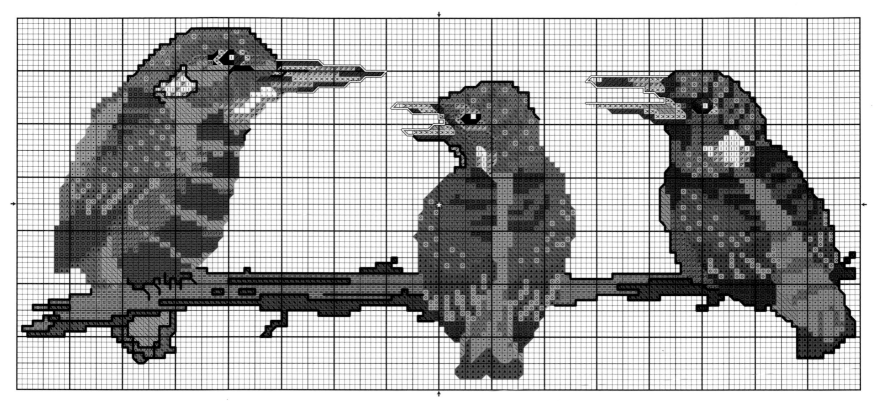

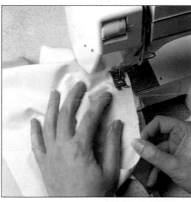

2 With right sides facing, pin the canvas bag front and back together. Machine stitch along the sides and the bottom edge with a 1 cm (½ in) seam. Press the seam. Stitch the lining sections together, but do not turn right side out.

3 To make the handles, fold each smaller canvas piece in half lengthwise with right sides facing. Machine stitch the long side, turn right side out and press. Position one handle on the front of the bag with the raw edges of the handle matching the raw top edge of the bag. Position the second handle on the back of the bag. Fold the handles against the body of the bag.

4 With right sides facing, insert the lining. Stitch the lining to the body, enclosing the handles with a 1 cm (½ in) seam. Leave a gap for turning. Pull the bag through the gap and pin, then tack (baste) and slip stitch the gap. Press the bag to finish.

Cross stitch in two strands

1 1	1 White
• •	167 Light turquoise
⧄	169 Mid turquoise
▣	170 Dark turquoise
▨	326 Rusty orange
▨	349 Caramel
═	379 Mid beige
■	403 Black
⋗ ⋗	858 Green grey
◇ ◇	875 Light forest green
◤	889 Dark brown
▽ ▽	900 Pearl grey
◪	1041 Dark slate grey
⟍ ⟍	1047 Light peach
И И	1048 Mid peach
∧ ∧	167/169 Blend light/mid turquoise
▲ ▲	877/779 Blend sea green/slate blue
Y Y	779 Slate blue/Kreinik sky blue HL

Backstitch in two strands

═══	1 White
━━━	403 Black

☆ Middle point

Fledglings picture

The sound of fledglings chirping from their nest, waiting for their parents to bring them food, is a sure sign of spring.

1 Work the design using two strands for cross stitch and one or two strands for backstitch as indicated in the key.

2 When the work is complete, check it for marks. If it is grubby, you can rinse the stitching in warm, soapy water.

3 Allow it to dry flat and press lightly with the stitching face down on a towel so that you don't flatten the stitches.

4 Mount your work by following the instructions for lacing a picture.

YOU WILL NEED
Design size: 83 x 118
fabric: 14 hpi Aida, 23 x 28 cm
    (9 x 11 in)
26 tapestry needle
stranded cotton, as listed in key
iron
towel
ruler
pencil
cardboard
wadding (batting)
scissors
pins
sharp needle
sewing thread
picture frame

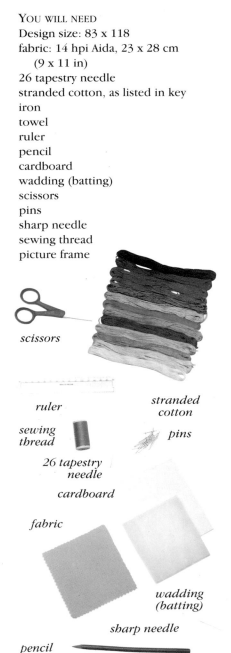

scissors

ruler

stranded cotton

sewing thread

pins

26 tapestry needle

cardboard

fabric

wadding (batting)

sharp needle

pencil

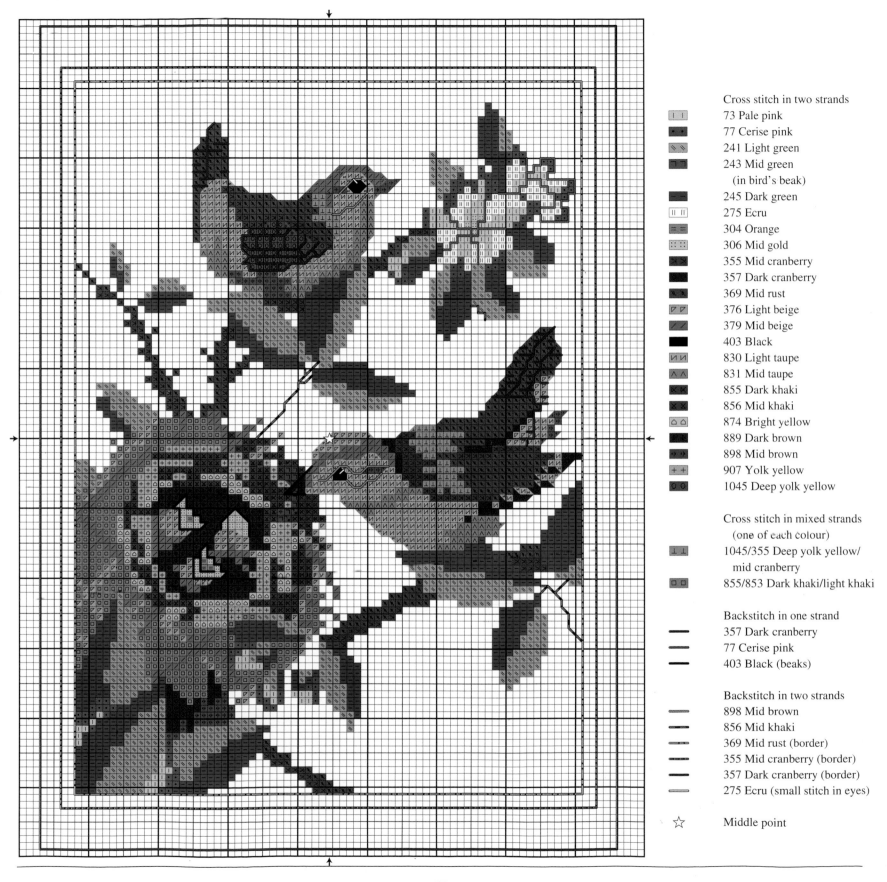

Cross stitch in two strands

| | | 73 Pale pink
| | 77 Cerise pink
| | 241 Light green
| | 243 Mid green
(in bird's beak)
| | 245 Dark green
| II II | 275 Ecru
| = = | 304 Orange
| : : : | 306 Mid gold
| > > | 355 Mid cranberry
| | 357 Dark cranberry
| | 369 Mid rust
| ▽ ▽ | 376 Light beige
| / / | 379 Mid beige
| | 403 Black
| Ͷ Ͷ | 830 Light taupe
| ∧ ∧ | 831 Mid taupe
| ⋉ ⋉ | 855 Dark khaki
| ⋈ ⋈ | 856 Mid khaki
| △ △ | 874 Bright yellow
| | 889 Dark brown
| ⊕ ⊕ | 898 Mid brown
| + + | 907 Yolk yellow
| ○ ○ | 1045 Deep yolk yellow

Cross stitch in mixed strands
(one of each colour)

| ⊥ ⊥ | 1045/355 Deep yolk yellow/
mid cranberry
| ▢ ▢ | 855/853 Dark khaki/light khaki

Backstitch in one strand

—— 357 Dark cranberry
—— 77 Cerise pink
—— 403 Black (beaks)

Backstitch in two strands

—— 898 Mid brown
—— 856 Mid khaki
—— 369 Mid rust (border)
—— 355 Mid cranberry (border)
—— 357 Dark cranberry (border)
—— 275 Ecru (small stitch in eyes)

☆ Middle point

Daffodil doorstop

Rich vibrant yellows can be found in abundance
when daffodils bloom; with their deep-hued
trumpets and paler leaves, they lend a
cheerfulness to every home.

YOU WILL NEED
Design size: 53 x 111
fabric: 14 hpi Aida, 16 x 27 cm
  (6¼ x 10½ in)
26 tapestry needle
stranded cotton as listed in key
brick
wadding (batting)
tape measure
scissors
pins
sharp needle
sewing thread
velvet

1 Work the cross stitch using two
strands throughout.

2 Backstitch the details as marked
on the chart, using one strand for each
of the colours.

3 Use two strands for the French
knots in the centre of each trumpet
using pale yellow thread.

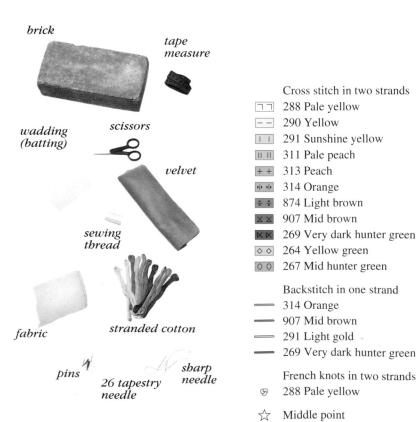

brick

tape measure

wadding (batting)

scissors

velvet

sewing thread

fabric

stranded cotton

pins

26 tapestry needle

sharp needle

Cross stitch in two strands
- 288 Pale yellow
- 290 Yellow
- 291 Sunshine yellow
- 311 Pale peach
- 313 Peach
- 314 Orange
- 874 Light brown
- 907 Mid brown
- 269 Very dark hunter green
- 264 Yellow green
- 267 Mid hunter green

Backstitch in one strand
- 314 Orange
- 907 Mid brown
- 291 Light gold
- 269 Very dark hunter green

French knots in two strands
- 288 Pale yellow

☆ Middle point

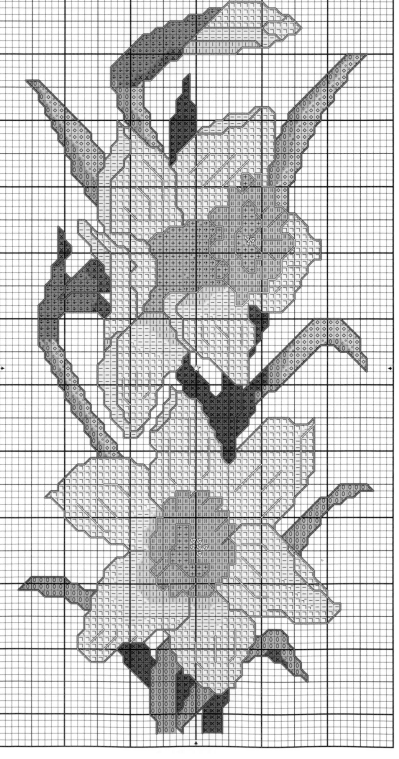

MAKING-UP INSTRUCTIONS

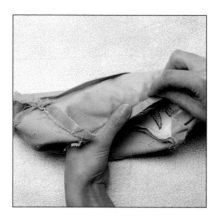

1 Cover the brick with wadding (batting) and tack (baste). Attach 10 cm (4 in) wide velvet strips along each edge of the design allowing 2.5 cm (1 in) extra.

2 With 1.5 cm (⅝ in) seam allowances, stitch the four velvet strips to the edges of the design, right sides together. Join the side seams.

3 Slip the cover over the brick so that all the edges are covered. Tack (baste) the final piece of velvet to the wide bottom of the brick, covering the bottom and slightly over the edges.

4 Turn under the edges of the cover and slip stitch it to the velvet covering the bottom of the brick.

Aconites sampler

The instantly recognizable yellows of the aconites
bring a touch of cheer to a wintry landscape.

YOU WILL NEED
Design size: 85 x 85
fabric: 28 hpi evenweave over two
    threads, 25 x 25 cm (10 x 10 in)
26 tapestry needle
stranded cotton, as listed in key
iron
towel
ruler
pencil
cardboard
wadding (batting)
scissors
pins
sharp needle
sewing thread
picture frame

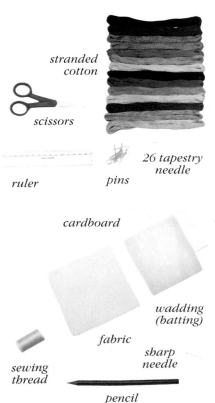

stranded cotton

scissors

ruler

pins

26 tapestry needle

cardboard

wadding (batting)

fabric

sharp needle

sewing thread

pencil

Cross stitch in two strands

	110 Dark lilac
	167 Light turquoise
	168 Dark turquoise
	205 Dark blue-green
	206 Light blue-green
	238 Bright green
	253 Light yellow-green
	254 Mid green
	288 Very pale yellow
	298 Deep yellow
	311 Light orange
	314 Dark orange
	358 Dark mink
	399 Grey
	295 Pale yellow
	13 Red
	90 Light lilac

Backstitch in one strand
358 Dark mink

French knot in one strand
403 Black

☆   Middle point

1 Work the design using two strands for cross stitch and one strand for backstitch and French knots.

2 When the work is complete, check it for marks. If it is grubby, you can rinse the stitching in warm, soapy water to remove any marks.

3 Allow it to dry flat and press lightly with the stitching face down on a towel so that you don't flatten the stitches.

4 Mount your work by following the instructions for lacing a picture.

Lavender needlecase

Keep all your needles safe in this beautiful needlecase, adding more felt pages if required. The lavender plant on the front is a typical Victorian design, but the border gives it a more contemporary look.

YOU WILL NEED
Design size: 80 x 90
fabric 26 hpi black evenweave
  20 x 30 cm (8 x 12 in)
sharp needle
tacking (basting) thread
ruler
26 tapestry needle
stranded cotton, as listed in key
iron
damp cloth
black iron-on interfacing,
  13 x 23 cm (5 x 9 in)
scissors
black felt, 30 x 30 cm (12 x 12 in)
pinking shears
sewing thread

iron-on interfacing

evenweave

tacking (basting) thread

sewing thread

needle

stranded cotton

1 Protect the edge of the canvas with buttonhole stitch. Fold the canvas in half lengthways. Tack (baste) a guide line down the fold line and another 9 cm (3½ in) from the right-hand side.

2 Cross stitch the border of the design first and then complete the lavender plant. Once complete, press on the wrong side with a damp cloth. Iron the interfacing into the middle of the wrong side of the canvas. Fold the canvas over the interfacing, mitre the corners and slip stitch to secure.

3 Cut out two 12 x 22 cm (4½ x 8½ in) rectangles of felt with pinking shears. Lay one piece of felt on top of the wrong side of the needlecase and attach using tiny backstitch. Sew the second piece along the centre fold line to complete.

Cross stitch in two strands

● ●	550 Dark purple
O O	208 Purple
+ +	210 Lilac
△ △	909 Dark green
▲ ▲	943 Blue green
□ □	912 Light green
✕ ✕	955 Mint green
◆ ◆	676 Gold
☆	Middle point

VARIATION
You can use the border design to make a small square matching pincushion.

Coasters and table mat

The Victorians made mats to cover nearly every surface in the house as most nineteenth-century furniture was French polished. This delightfully simple cross-stitch design is ideal to decorate the table for supper in the evening and could be worked on ready-made table linen.

YOU WILL NEED
Design size: 50 x 50
fabric: evenweave linen, 36 x 50 cm
    (14 x 20 in)
ruler
scissors
26 tapestry needle
stranded cotton, as listed on key
tacking (basting) thread

ruler

scissors

stranded cotton

tacking (basting) thread

26 tapestry needle

evenweave linen

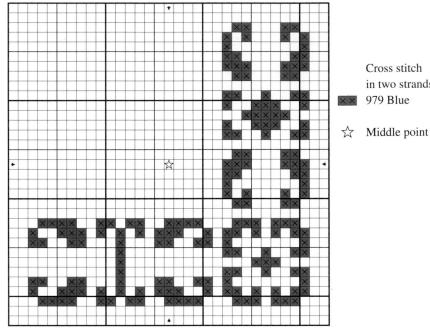

Cross stitch
in two strands

× × 979 Blue

☆ Middle point

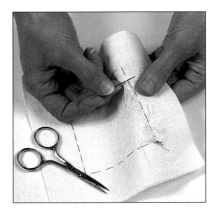

1 Cut two 13 cm (5 in) squares for the coasters and a 25 x 36 cm (10 x 14 in) rectangle for the mat. Tack (baste) a line 2.5 cm (1 in) in from each edge of all the pieces. Beginning in the middle of each side, draw out six threads as far as the tacking (basting) line.

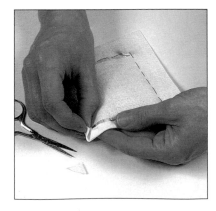

2 Mitre the corners and fold over a 1 cm (½ in) hem on all sides.

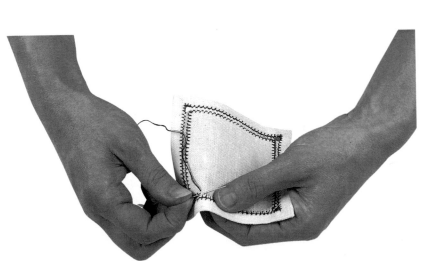

3 Work hem stitch along the outside edge of each piece. Group the threads in bundles of four and catch in the hem turning at the same time. Work hem stitch on the inside edge of the drawn threads, sewing two threads from one group with two from the next to form a zig-zag effect. Work buttonhole stitch in the corners and sew a small spider's web across the square gap.

4 Tack (baste) guide lines in the corners of the coasters and mat, 2.5 cm (1 in) from the edge. Work the cross-stitch design, remove tacking (basting) threads and press on the wrong side.

Poppy doorplate

A doorplate keeps fingerprints at bay. By enclosing an attractive embroidery inside you can add decoration in a practical way.

YOU WILL NEED
Design size: 22 x 124
fabric: 14 hpi Aida, 12 x 29 cm
  (4¾ x 11½ in)
26 tapestry needle
stranded cotton, as listed in key
craft doorplate
scissors
cardboard

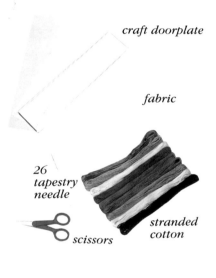

craft doorplate

fabric

26 tapestry needle

scissors

stranded cotton

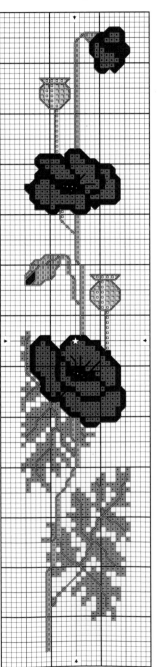

Cross stitch in two strands		Backstitch in one strand	
▪▪▪	403 Black	——	403 Black
•••	1025 Light coral red	——	844 Dark fern green
▪▪▪	47 Dark red	——	45 Very dark garnet
□□□	305 Light yellow beige	——	309 Dark beige brown
⌐⌐⌐	306 Dark yellow beige		
‖‖‖	254 Mid green	☆	Middle point
►►►	844 Dark fern green		

1 Work the cross stitch using two strands throughout.

2 Backstitch the details, using one strand in each colour.

3 Neatly finish the work. Cut the design to the same size as the doorplate, place behind the plate with the design facing through the glass, and secure in place with a piece of backing cardboard cut to the same size as the doorplate.

Garden card

With the sun shining relentlessly down on your garden, who can blame the bird for looking for a refreshing drink? Stitch this card for your favourite garden enthusiast.

You will need
Design size: 35 x 39
fabric: 18 hpi Aida, 12 x 12 cm
  (4¾ x 4¾ in)
26 tapestry needle
stranded cotton, as listed in key
card with opening
wadding (batting)
fabric-marker pen
scissors
double-sided tape

1 Work the cross stitch using two strands throughout.

2 Backstitch the detail, using one strand, for each colour.

3 Neatly finish the work and mount it by following the instructions for filling a card.

stranded cotton

card with opening

scissors

wadding (batting)

fabric-marker pen

26 tapestry needle

fabric

Cross stitch in two strands
● ●	403	Black
⊓ ⊓	292	Light lemon
– –	297	Buttercup yellow
I I	373	Tan
+ +	281	Dark olive
✕ ✕	280	Olive
⊠ ⊠	390	Cream
∧ ∧	398	Pearl grey
и и	399	Mid grey
⊁ ⊁	273	Grey
○ ○	98	Mauve
↓ ↓	25	Rose pink
← ←	268	Dark hunter green
✱ ✱	265	Light green

Backstitch in one strand
——	403	Black
——	268	Dark hunter green
——	375	Beige
——	273	Grey
——	98	Mauve
——	25	Rose pink
☆	Middle point	

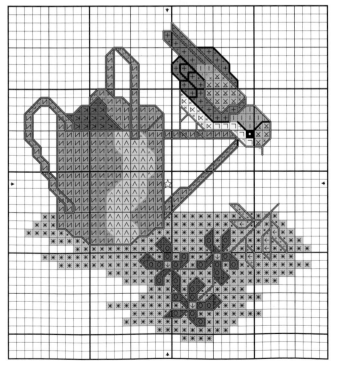

Summer cushion

Garlands of summer flowers spring from this bright and cheerful design. It's a fabulous project for an experienced needleworker who is looking for a challenge.

YOU WILL NEED
Design size: 154 x 156
fabric: 14hpi Aida, 36 x 36 cm
  (14 x 14 in)
26 tapestry needle
stranded cotton, as listed in key
backing fabric
tape measure
fabric-marker pen
scissors
pins
sharp needle
sewing thread
thimble
cushion pad

backing fabric

26 tapestry needle

tape measure

fabric-marker pen

scissors

thimble

stranded cotton

pins

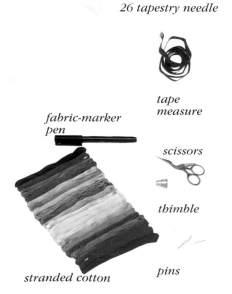

Cross stitch in two strands

● ●	403 Black
⁄ ⁄	398 Pearl grey
⅃ ⅃	397 Pale grey
▮ ▮	380 Dark brown
+ +	340 Red brown
÷ ÷	347 Fawn
⊹ ⊹	290 Dark lemon
⋉ ⋉	289 Yellow
⨯ ⨯	292 Light lemon
Z Z	185 Eau de nil
⋁ ⋁	256 Mid grass green
⋮⋮	244 Grass green
○ ○	246 Deep pine green
← ←	142 Bright blue
↑ ↑	133 Ultramarine
▶ ▶	102 Dark purple
↗ ↗	96 Lilac
⬇ ⬇	44 Dark maroon pink
→ →	42 Light maroon
▶ ▶	62 Dark pink
✳ ✳	25 Rose pink
⅃ ⅃	8 Mid salmon
■ ■	46 Berry red
△ △	332 Orange red

Backstitch in one strand

—— 102 Dark purple
—— 62 Dark pink
—— 403 Black

French knots in two strands
♥ 102 Dark purple

☆ Middle point

1 Begin the cross stitch at the centre of the design and work the cross stitch in two strands throughout.

2 Backstitch details, using one strand, throughout.

3 Decorate the fuchsia with French knots using two strands. Neatly finish the work and make up into a cushion, following the instructions for the Spring cushion.

Summer garland

If you're new to cross stitch, this charming garland design will suit even a novice stitcher. Whole cross stitch with backstitch detail make up this elegant and simple design.

YOU WILL NEED
Design size: 37 x 33
fabric: 28 hpi evenweave over
  two threads, 15 x 12 cm
  (6 x 4½ in)
26 tapestry needle
stranded cotton, as listed in key
crystal (glass) pot
fabric-marker pen
scissors
wadding (batting)

1 Work the cross stitch using two strands throughout.

2 Backstitch the detail, using one strand, in each colour.

3 Neatly finish the design and mount it by following the instructions for filling a pot.

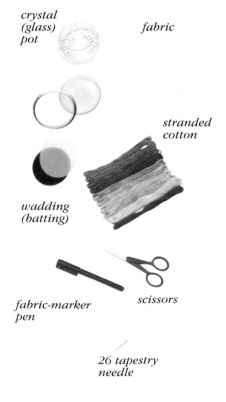

crystal (glass) pot

fabric

stranded cotton

wadding (batting)

fabric-marker pen

scissors

26 tapestry needle

Cross stitch in two strands

· ·	342	Pale mauve pink
\\ \\	109	Light violet
↑↑	101	Mid purple
↓ ↓	23	Salmon pink
✳✳	9	Dark salmon
⊓⊓	10	Coral red
⊐⊐	210	Bright green
I I	876	Pale sage green
◀◀	281	Deep khaki
▶▶	48	Pale pink
• •	292	Buttermilk

Backstitch in one strand

——	281	Grass green
——	10	Dark rose pink
——	210	Bright green
——	101	Mid purple
——	236	Dark charcoal

☆ Middle point

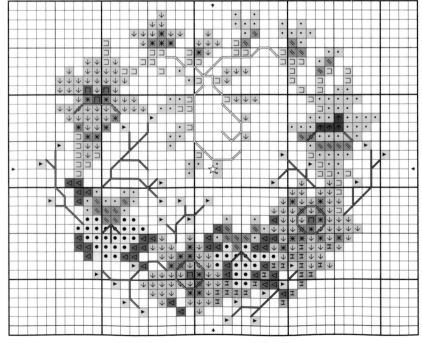

Butterfly gift tags

Flitting from bloom to bloom, the butterfly is a familiar sight during the summer months. Wrap a summer gift and add a delicate tag to give a personal touch.

YOU WILL NEED
Design size: 21 x 21 and 20 x 20
fabric: 18 hpi Aida, 16 x 9 cm
  (6¼ x 3½ in)
26 tapestry needle
stranded cotton, as listed in key
gift tags with openings
wadding (batting)
fabric-marker pen
scissors
double-sided tape

1 Work the cross stitch using two strands throughout.

2 Backstitch the detail, using one strand for each colour.

3 Neatly finish the work, and mount in a gift tag by following the instructions for filling a card.

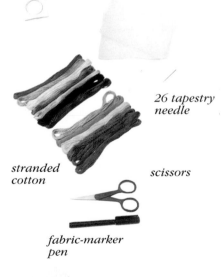

gift tag

wadding (batting)

26 tapestry needle

stranded cotton

scissors

fabric-marker pen

fabric

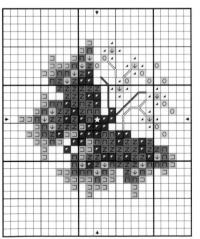

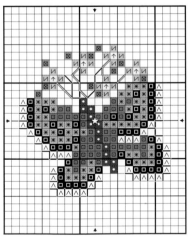

Cross stitch in two strands

⊐⊐	313 Light orange
⊓⊓	310 Light brown
↓↓	314 Orange
ZZ	332 Orange red
◢◥	380 Dark brown
◢◢	291 Sunshine yellow
OO	260 Moss green
◖●◗	236 Dark charcoal
□□	403 Black
▣▣	131 Cornflower blue
＊＊	145 Periwinkle blue
⊠⊠	281 Deep leaf green
∧∧	1 White
ИИ	108 Lilac
↑↑	361 Apricot

Backstitch in one strand

───	380 Dark brown
━━━	403 Black
══	281 Deep leaf green
══	260 Leaf green
☆	Middle point

Summer cottage

Tucked away at the end of a country lane, a summer cottage, with its abundant garden, makes a welcome oasis in the calm of the countryside. Bring it to life with this wonderful romantic cottage design.

1 Work the cross stitch in two strands throughout.

2 Backstitch the detail using one strand throughout. Work French knots in one strand for the rosebuds and small flowers.

3 Finish the work and mount it by following the instructions for lacing a frame.

YOU WILL NEED
Design size: 106 x 76
fabric: 30 hpi linen over two
  threads, 26 x 19 cm
  (10¼ x 7½ in)
26 tapestry needle
stranded cotton, as listed in key
picture frame
cardboard
tape measure
fabric-marker pen
scissors
wadding (batting)
pins
sharp needle
sewing thread

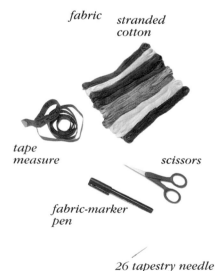

fabric
stranded cotton
tape measure
scissors
fabric-marker pen
26 tapestry needle
wadding (batting)

Cross stitch in two strands			
131 Cornflower blue	352 Very dark mahogany	===== 1216 Variegated green	French knots in one strand
1011 Salmon pink	1216 Variegated green	===== 1208 Variegated purple	● 352 Very dark mahogany
292 Light lemon	297 Bright yellow	===== 1201 Variegated rose	● 1208 Variegated purple
28 Fuchsia		===== 292 Cream	● 131 Cornflower blue
266 Light hunter green	Backstitch in one strand	===== 297 Buttercup yellow	
259 Light green	—— 403 Black	===== 266 Light hunter green	☆ Middle point
	—— 352 Very dark mahogany	===== 1208/1210 Variegated purple/variegated blue	

Summer roses hat band

Add a touch of elegance to your summer hat by adding a decorative floral border. Repeat a single design for added effect, and you'll be the belle of the garden party.

YOU WILL NEED

Design size: 48 x 26 repeat
fabric: 14 hpi Aida band,
   measure around the hat, plus
   3 cm (1¼ in)
stranded cotton, as listed in key
26 tapestry needle
hat
tape measure
pins
scissors
sharp needle
sewing thread

hat

stranded cotton

scissors

*tape
measure*

*sharp
needle*

Aida band

pins

*26 tapestry
needle*

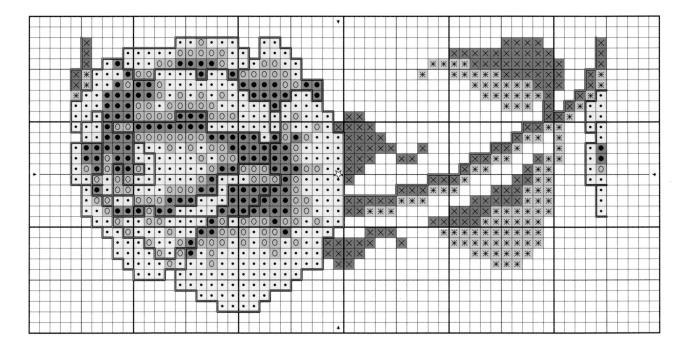

1 Work the cross stitch using two strands throughout.

2 Work the backstitch detail, using one strand throughout.

Cross stich in two strands

· ·	49 Light pink
o o	55 Mid pink
● ●	62 Dark pink
✕ ✕	216 Light green
✳ ✳	214 Leaf green

Backstitch in one strand

—— 78 Light raspberry
—— 216 Light green

☆ Middle point

MAKING-UP INSTRUCTIONS

1 Measure the circumference of your hat and then divide the total measurement by two to get the centrepoint for the design. Using this measurement, mark the centre of the design on your band with a pin.

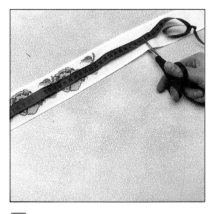

2 Work the design stitching your first repeat from the centrepoint. Continue repeating the flower design to fit around the crown of the hat. Using the centre point as a mid measurement, cut the band to length allowing 5 cm (2 in) at either end for finishing.

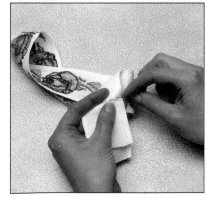

3 Place right sides together and stitch. Leave a 1.5 cm (⅝ in) seam allowance and press the seam flat. Turn the right way out and fit on to your hat with the seam at the back.

VARIATION

You can use any detail from the designs in this book to make pretty edgings for tablecloths, towels and napkins.

Rainbow bookmark

Save your page with this striking array of rainbow colours. A bookmark is both useful and attractive and it is an easy project for the cross stitcher.

YOU WILL NEED
Design size: 87 x 30
fabric: 18 hpi Aida, 20 x 7.5 cm
    (8 x 3 in)
26 tapestry needle
stranded cotton, as listed in key
iron
scissors
sewing thread
sharp needle
felt
pins

stranded cotton

sewing thread

scissors

fabric

felt

26 tapestry needle

pins

needle

1 Work the design using two strands for all the cross stitch except the rainbow, which uses two strands for the bottom stitch and one strand for the top stitch. Work all the backstitch in one strand. Press the long edges of the embroidered piece to the wrong side and trim to within four squares of the fold line.

2 Using small neat stitches, hand sew a strip of felt on to the back of the embroidery, ensuring it is equidistant from both ends.

3 Machine stitch through the Aida and the felt, seven squares from each short edge of the embroidery.

4 Trim the Aida 10 squares away from the machine-stitched line. Next, remove the threads along the short edges of the bookmark to six squares deep to make a fringe.

Cross stitch in two strands for lower stitch and one strand of 928 for top stitch

■■	1006 Red		▲▲	238 Bright green
⊞⊞	314 Orange		◇◇	142 Dark blue
↑↑	291 Yellow		▼▼	101 Dark violet

Cross stitch in two strands

··	2 White
■■	254 Mid green
⁄⁄	259 Light green
｜｜	266 Light hunter green
++	314 Orange
⊞⊞	1006 Red
▽▽	928 Light blue

Backstitch using one strand

—	266 Dark green
—	403 Black

☆	Middle point

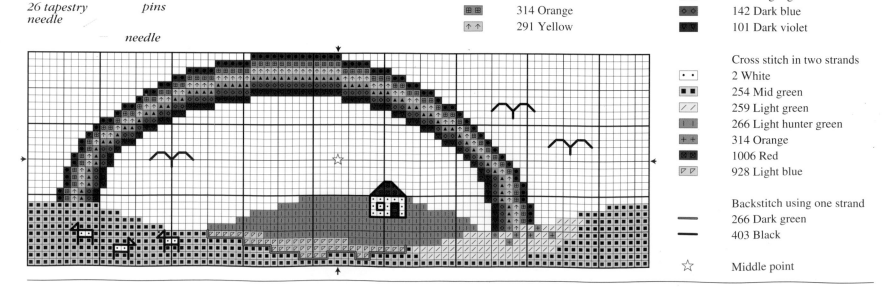

Ladybird paperweight

You could use this paperweight to keep your kitchen notes and recipes tidy. The ladybird is a versatile motif; use the design to decorate a shelf border and coordinate the room.

YOU WILL NEED
Design size: 32 x 33
fabric: 14 hpi Aida, 13 x 13 cm
(5 x 5 in)
26 tapestry needle
stranded cotton, as listed in key
8 cm (3 in) craft paperweight
pencil
scissors

1 First work the design using two strands for cross stitch and one strand for backstitch.

2 When complete, draw around the piece of felt supplied with the paperweight on to your design. Ensure the motif is centred.

3 Cut neatly around the drawn line on the embroidered piece.

4 Place the embroidery under the weight with the design facing into the glass and finish by placing the sticky felt on the bottom.

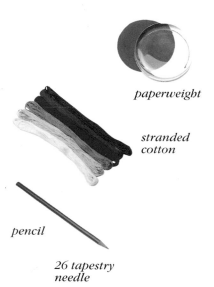

paperweight

stranded cotton

pencil

26 tapestry needle

scissors   *fabric*

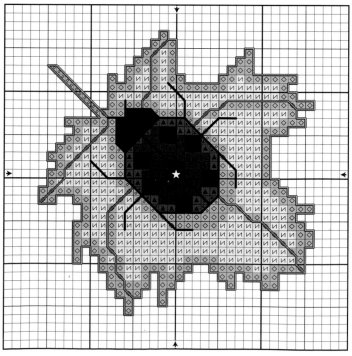

Cross stitch in two strands
 259 Light green
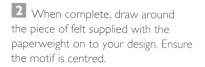 265 Very light hunter green
335 Light red
403 Black
9046 Dark red

Backstitch in one strand
— 268 Dark hunter green
— 403 Black

☆ Middle point

Bees padded coat hanger

Covered coat hangers help to stop delicate
garments being snagged and pulled out of shape.
This busy bees design makes an elegant hanger.

YOU WILL NEED
Design size: 215 x 41
fabric: 28 hpi evenweave over two
    threads, 50 x 15 cm (20 x 6 in)
26 tapestry needle
stranded cotton, as listed in key
pencil
scissors
backing fabric
wadding (batting)
pins
120 cm (48 in) of 1 cm (½ in) lace
sharp needle
sewing thread
coat hanger
6 mm (¼ in) satin ribbon
double-sided tape

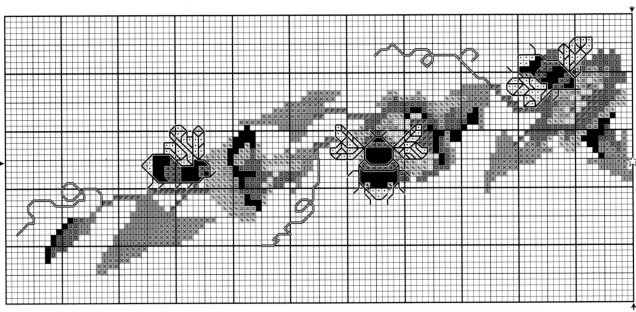

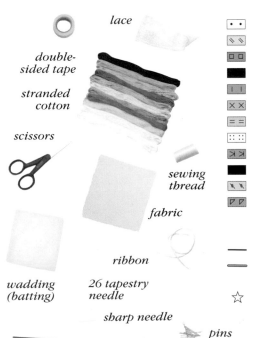

lace

double-sided tape

stranded cotton

scissors

sewing thread

fabric

ribbon

wadding (batting)

26 tapestry needle

sharp needle

pins

pencil

Cross stitch in two strands

··	1 White
�	128 Sky blue
□□	130 Blue
■	127 Royal blue
			204 Green
××	214 Mid green
==	274 Pastel blue
::: :::	293 Yellow
>>	303 Orange
■	403 Black
＼＼	891 Dark yellow
▽▽	943 Light brown

Backstitch in one strand

— 403 Black
— 204 Green

☆ Middle point

MAKING-UP INSTRUCTIONS

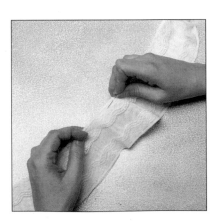

1 First work the design, reversing the
pattern to make the second half. Make a
template from the hanger and use this as
a guide to cut hanger shapes from the
embroidered fabric, the backing fabric
and two pieces of wadding (batting).

2 Pin the length of lace to the backing
fabric with right sides facing and raw
edges matching. Gather the lace a little
around the corners if necessary. Tack
(baste) and sew.

3 With right sides facing, place the embroidered fabric on top of the laced backing fabric. Lay a piece of wadding (batting) on each side and tack (baste) into position. Stitch around the lower edge and curves, leaving the top edge open. Trim the wadding (batting), clip the corners and turn to the right side.

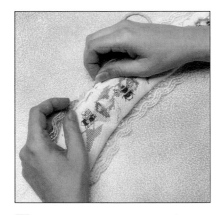

4 Bind the hanger hook with ribbon by applying a piece of double-sided tape to the top of the hook. Work ribbon over this and tape the opposite end of the ribbon to the hanger. Insert the hanger into the cover, turn under the raw edges and close the top edges by slip stitching them together.

Heron card

Inspired by an original watercolour, this special greetings card has been designed for you to stitch and give to a deserving friend.

YOU WILL NEED
Design size: 60 x 97
fabric: 18 hpi Aida, 12 x 17 cm
   (4$\frac{1}{2}$ x 6$\frac{1}{2}$ in)
26 tapestry needle
stranded cotton, as listed in key
iron
towel
card with opening
pencil
wadding (batting)
scissors
double-sided tape

stranded cotton

card with opening

fabric

wadding (batting)

scissors

26 tapestry needle

double-sided tape

pencil

1 Starting from the centre of the design, work the heron using one strand throughout.

2 When the work is complete, check it for marks. If it is grubby, you can rinse the stitching in warm, soapy water.

3 Allow it to dry flat and press lightly with the stitching face down on a towel so that you don't flatten the stitches.

4 Mount your work by following the instructions for filling a card.

Cross stitch in one strand
| | | 1 White
■ 403 Black
218 Dark green
→ → 214 Mid green
266 Hunter green
381 Dark brown
▽ ▽ 295 Pale yellow
+ + 891 Dark yellow
⊳ ⊳ 235 Dark grey
◇ ◇ 234 Light grey
∕ ∕ 399 Mid grey
= = 274 Pastel blue
850 Mid grey-blue

Backstitch in one strand
236 Very dark grey
403 Black
399 Mid grey
891 Dark yellow
381 Dark brown

French knot in one strand
● 236 Very dark grey

☆ Middle point

Rabbit coaster

Wildlife subjects are always popular and the rabbit is a particular favourite. You're sure to get a smile from friends when you present them with a set of these charming coasters.

YOU WILL NEED
Design size: 37 x 32
fabric: 18 hpi Aida, 10 x 10 cm
   (4 x 4 in)
26 tapestry needle
stranded cotton, as listed in key
8 cm (3 in) craft coaster
pencil
scissors

1 First work the design using one strand throughout.

2 When complete, draw around the piece of felt supplied with the coaster on to your design, centring the motif under the felt.

3 Cut neatly around the drawn line on the design.

4 Place the embroidery face upwards in the coaster. Finish by placing the sticky felt on the back.

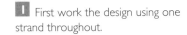
stranded cotton

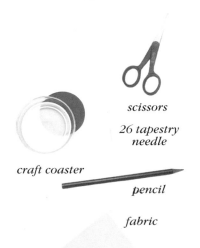
craft coaster

scissors

26 tapestry needle

pencil

fabric

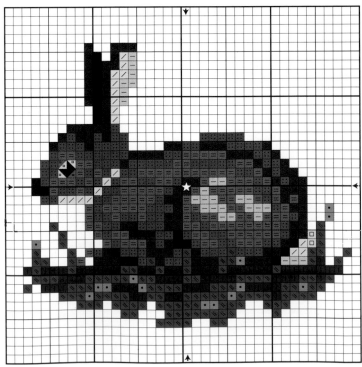

Cross stitch in one strand

◼	269 Very dark hunter green
⬚	266 Hunter green
◩	268 Dark hunter green
□□	2 Ecru
− −	368 Deep cream
∕ ∕	276 Mid cream
═ ═	370 Mid mink
▦	358 Dark mink
◼	380 Dark brown
◼	382 Chocolate brown
☆	Middle point

Hedgehog pot

Even though a real hedgehog's back is covered in unwelcoming prickly spines, a sewn hedgehog always looks cute. Our cuddly hedgehog looks super mounted in the lid of a useful trinket pot.

YOU WILL NEED
Design size: 39 x 24
fabric: 18 hpi Aida, 10 x 10 cm
    (4 x 4 in)
26 tapestry needle
stranded cotton, as listed in key
iron
towel
7 cm (2½ in) craft pot
pencil
scissors
wadding (batting)

1 Starting from the centre of the design, work the hedgehog using two strands throughout.

2 When the work is complete, check it for marks. If it is grubby, you can rinse the stitching in warm, soapy water.

3 Allow it to dry flat and press lightly with the stitching face down on a towel so that you don't flatten the stitches.

4 Mount your work by following the instructions for filling a pot.

stranded cotton

pot

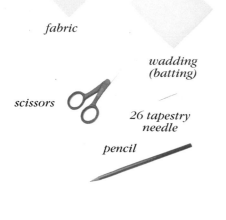

fabric

wadding (batting)

scissors

26 tapestry needle

pencil

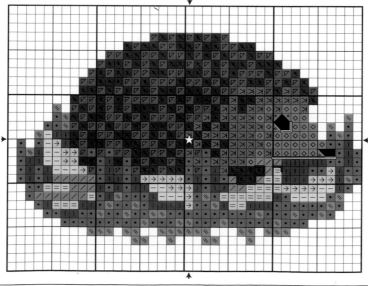

Cross stitch in two strands
269 Very dark hunter green
268 Dark hunter green
266 Hunter green
907 Sage green
874 Light sage green
365 Mid rust
363 Light tan
403 Black
379 Mid mink
400 Slate grey
382 Chocolate brown
236 Dark grey

Backstitch in two strands
403 Black
382 Chocolate brown

☆ Middle point

Peacock book cover

Capture the essence of the regal yet flamboyant peacock by decorating this original book cover with beads and blended threads.

YOU WILL NEED
Design size: 90 x 120
fabric: 14 hpi Aida, 36 x 90 cm
    (14 x 36 in)
sharp needle
sewing thread
24 tapestry needle
Kreinik thread, as listed in key
embroidery frame
glass beads
hardback book
tape measure
pencil
scissors
iron
small crochet hook

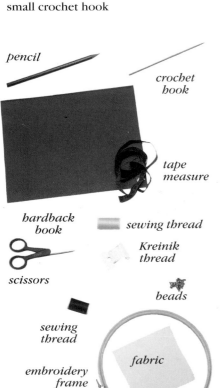

pencil

crochet hook

tape measure

hardback book

sewing thread

Kreinik thread

scissors

beads

sewing thread

fabric

embroidery frame

needle

MAKING-UP INSTRUCTIONS

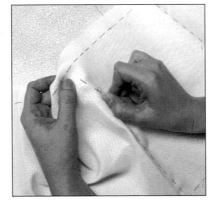

1 Mark up the fabric for stitching. Tack (baste) a line 20 cm (8 in) from the right-hand edge. Work the design using one strand of Kreinik thread throughout.

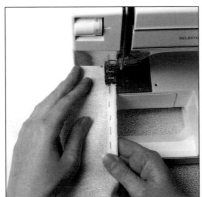

2 Measure the fabric needed for the book cover to include two pockets. Trim the excess fabric, leaving 4 cm (1¹/₂ in) for hems. Machine stitch the hems all round, turning under 2 cm (³/₄ in) twice. Clip the corners and oversew them.

3 Fold the fabric at the front edge to make a pocket and slip stitch along the top and bottom edges. Press the cover, then wrap it around the book. Fold the fabric into the back cover to make the back pocket. Slip stitch along the edges.

4 Make two 55 cm (21¹/₂ in) long cords by crocheting chains using three strands of Kreinik threads. Thread beads on to the ends of the chains, finish with a series of knots and attach to the top and bottom of the inside of the fabric cover.

Cross stitch in one strand
- Kreinik fine braid (#8) - 002
- Kreinik fine braid (#8) - 009
- Kreinik fine braid (#8) - 005
- Kreinik fine braid (#8) - 008
- Kreinik fine braid (#8) - 008 +002

Backstitch in one strand
- Kreinik fine braid (#8) - 005

Beading
- Mill Hill glass seed beads 62013

Cross stitch twice in the same holes in one strand
- Kreinik fine braid (#8) - 051

☆ Middle point

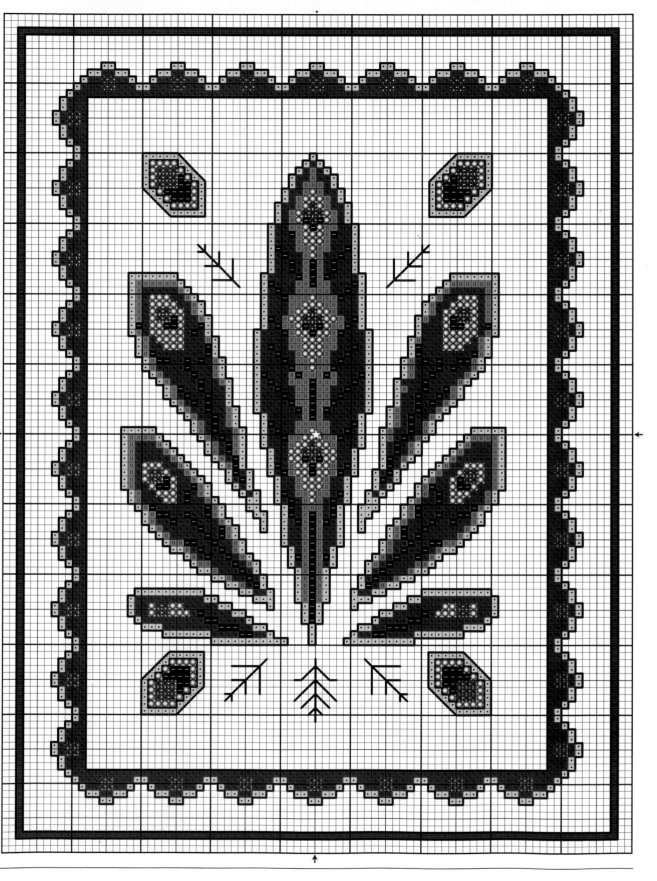

TIP

When adding beads to a design, use a beading needle threaded with sewing thread. Begin stitching as if you were making a half cross stitch, but before taking the needle back through the fabric, push a single bead through the needle and on to the thread. Put the needle back through the fabric to finish the half cross stitch. Work the next stitch.

Summer sampler

Remind yourself of a perfect summer by stitching this crowded sampler full of everything special from the season. If you prefer, you could work the elements separately and mount them in a card.

YOU WILL NEED
Design size: 111 x 139
fabric: 28 hpi evenweave over
  two threads, 27 x 31 cm
  (10½ x 12¼ in)
26 tapestry needle
stranded cotton, as listed in key
picture frame
cardboard
tape measure
fabric-marker pen
scissors
wadding (batting)
pins
sharp needle
sewing thread

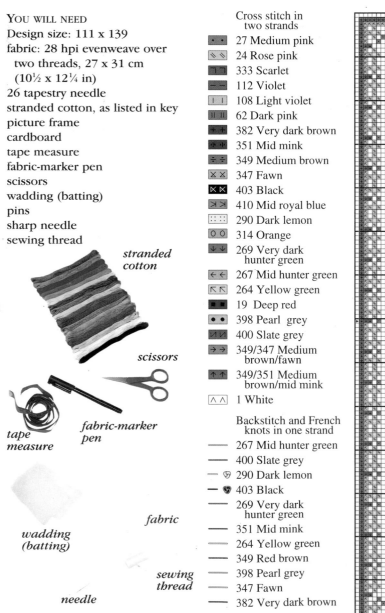

stranded cotton

scissors

tape measure

fabric-marker pen

wadding (batting)

fabric

sewing thread

needle

Cross stitch in
two strands

⟨•·•⟩	27 Medium pink
⟨＼＼⟩	24 Rose pink
⟨ˉˉ⟩	333 Scarlet
⟨ˉ⟩	112 Violet
⟨ǀ ǀ⟩	108 Light violet
⟨ǁ ǁ⟩	62 Dark pink
⟨＋＋⟩	382 Very dark brown
⟨◆◆⟩	351 Mid mink
⟨÷ ÷⟩	349 Medium brown
⟨✕ ✕⟩	347 Fawn
⟨✕ ✕⟩	403 Black
⟨＞ ＞⟩	410 Mid royal blue
⟨∷∷⟩	290 Dark lemon
⟨○ ○⟩	314 Orange
⟨↓ ↓⟩	269 Very dark hunter green
⟨← ←⟩	267 Mid hunter green
⟨↖ ↖⟩	264 Yellow green
⟨■ ■⟩	19 Deep red
⟨● ●⟩	398 Pearl grey
⟨Ⅳ Ⅳ⟩	400 Slate grey
⟨→ →⟩	349/347 Medium brown/fawn
⟨↑ ↑⟩	349/351 Medium brown/mid mink
⟨∧ ∧⟩	1 White

Backstitch and French
knots in one strand

——	267 Mid hunter green
——	400 Slate grey
═ ⊛	290 Dark lemon
— ⬤	403 Black
——	269 Very dark hunter green
——	351 Mid mink
——	264 Yellow green
········	349 Red brown
——	398 Pearl grey
——	347 Fawn
——	382 Very dark brown
☆	Middle point

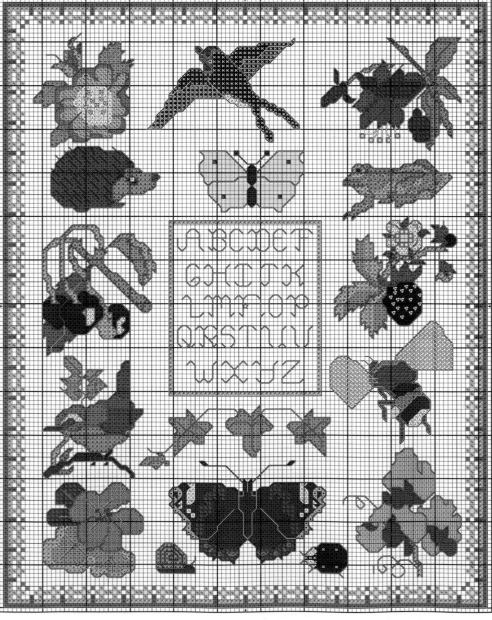

1 Work the cross stitch in two strands throughout.

2 Backstitch the details marked on the chart, using one strand for each colour.

3 Neatly finish the work and lace it, by following the instructions for lacing a frame.

Summer house

In the middle of the garden sits the summer house, a glass retreat surrounded by flowers. It is a relaxing, peaceful haven where you can sit and watch the world go by.

YOU WILL NEED
Design size: 49 x 60
fabric: 14 hpi Aida, 16 x 19 cm
 (6¼ x 7½ in)
26 tapestry needle
stranded cotton, as listed in key
card with opening
wadding (batting)
fabric-marker pen
scissors
double-sided tape

1 Work the cross stitch using two strands throughout.

2 Backstitch the detail on the chart, using one strand for each colour.

3 Neatly finish off the work and mount it by following the instructions for filling a card.

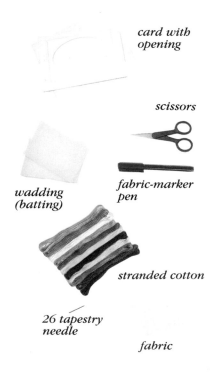

card with opening

scissors

wadding (batting)

fabric-marker pen

26 tapestry needle

stranded cotton

fabric

Cross stitch in two strands

◼◼	101 Mid purple
△△	943 Mid ochre
▲▲	62 Dark pink
I I	264 Yellow green
◼◼	9046 Bright red
↑↑	289 Yellow
∧∧	243 Mid green
ИИ	118 Mid mauve
II II	886 Beige
ƎƎ	374 Deep ochre
✳✳	274 Pearl grey

Backstitch in one strand
——— 360 Brown
——— 243 Mid green

☆ Middle point

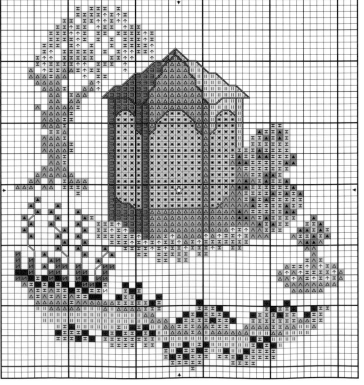

Collector's roses

A collector's cabinet provides ideal storage for your personal trinkets. Enhance it with this enchanting summer rose design for a truly superb display.

YOU WILL NEED
Design size: 39 x 39
fabric: 28 hpi evenweave over
  two threads, 15 x 15 cm
  (6 x 6 in)
26 tapestry needle
stranded cotton, as listed in key
yellow beads
craft display cabinet
cardboard
tape measure
fabric-marker pen
scissors
wadding (batting)
sharp needle
sewing thread
glue

1 Work cross stitch using two strands.

2 Backstitch the detail on the chart, using one strand for each colour. Stitch yellow beads for the ends of the stamens and stitch French knots in black on the end of the butterfly's antennae.

3 Finish the work. Cut the cardboard and wadding (batting) to the size of the cabinet insert. Wrap the design over the cardboard and wadding (batting), following the instructions for lacing a frame. Glue into the collector's cabinet.

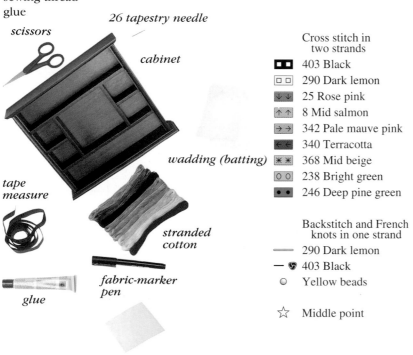

scissors
26 tapestry needle
cabinet
wadding (batting)
tape measure
stranded cotton
glue
fabric-marker pen
fabric

Cross stitch in
two strands

▉▉	403 Black
☐☐	290 Dark lemon
↓↓	25 Rose pink
↑↑	8 Mid salmon
→→	342 Pale mauve pink
←←	340 Terracotta
✳✳	368 Mid beige
○○	238 Bright green
••	246 Deep pine green

Backstitch and French
knots in one strand

—— 290 Dark lemon
—❧ 403 Black
○ Yellow beads

☆ Middle point

Country flowers scissors case

Keep your embroidery scissors safe inside this easy-to-make scissors case. Cornflowers and buttercups will make an heirloom case to keep the blades clean and sharp forever.

YOU WILL NEED
Design size: 26 x 44
fabric: 28 hpi evenweave over
  two threads, 24 x 15 cm
  (9½ x 6 in)
stranded cotton, as listed in key
26 tapestry needle
lining fabric, 18 x 20 cm (7 x 8 in)
tape measure
scissors
sharp needle
sewing thread
lightweight iron-on interfacing
iron
pins

1 Work the cross stitch using two strands throughout.

2 Backstitch detail, using one strand for each colour.

Cross stitch in two strands

+ +	109	Light violet
∧ ∧	253	Pale yellow green
И И	289	Yellow
\ \	62	Dark pink
⁄ ⁄	148	Dark cornflower blue
↓ ↓	266	Light hunter green
⥱ ⥱	127	Royal navy

Backstitch in one strand

— 150 Dark blue
— 267 Mid hunter green
— 69 Mauve
═ 298 Yellow

☆ Middle point

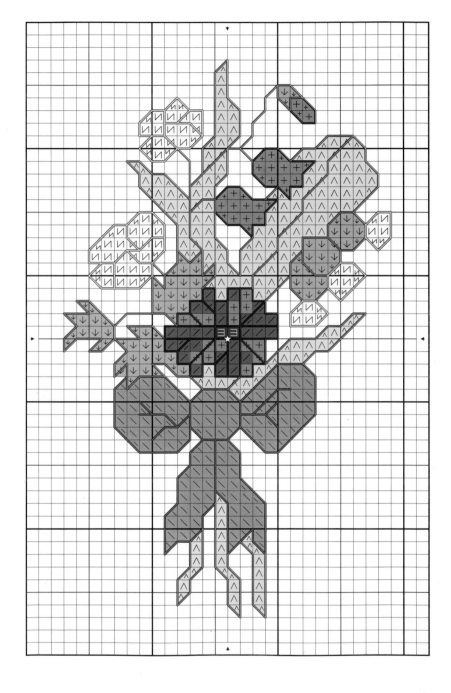

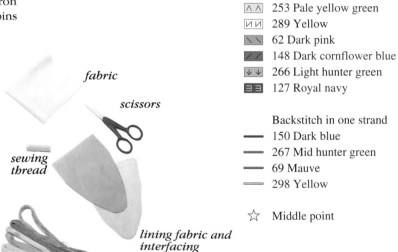

fabric

scissors

sewing thread

lining fabric and interfacing

stranded cotton

26 tapestry needle sharp needle

pins

MAKING-UP INSTRUCTIONS

1 Cut two pairs of lining and even-weave – triangular with the top edge 7.5 cm (3 in) and the length 10 cm (4 in), with 2 cm (¾ in) extra on all sides. Work the design centrally on one piece of evenweave. Iron on interfacing to the back of all pieces. Pin one lining and backing piece right sides together and stitch along top edge, 1.5 cm (⅝ in) in. Do the same with remaining lining and front piece. Press both pieces flat with seams open.

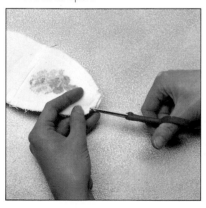

2 Pin the two pieces with right sides together and stitch around edge leaving approximately 4 cm (1½ in) gap at bottom of lining to allow for turning. Clip curves all along the edges.

3 Turn the work right side out and sew up the opening by hand with invisible stitches.

SEWING TIP
If you sew a piece of ribbon to either end of the scissor case, you can hang it around your neck and need never lose your scissors again.

Lilac print

The lilac tree attracts the most beautiful butterflies. From cabbage white to red admiral you'll be sure to find them hovering amongst the scented flowers of the lilac.

YOU WILL NEED
Design size: 68 x 86
fabric: 28 hpi evenweave over
   two threads, 18 x 22 cm
   (7 x 8½ in)
26 tapestry needle
stranded cotton, as listed in key
picture frame
cardboard
tape measure
fabric-marker pen
scissors
wadding (batting)
pins
sharp needle
sewing thread

1 Work the cross stitch using two strands throughout.

2 Backstitch the detail on the charts, using one strand for each colour.

3 Neatly finish the work. and mount it by following the instructions for lacing a frame.

Cross stitch in two strands

◄ ◄ 403 Black
► ► 11 Coral red
○ ○ 289 Yellow
● ● 243 Mid green
↑ ↑ 264 Yellow green
↓ ↓ 943 Mid brown
→ → 872 Deep lilac
□ □ 870 Lilac
||| 101 Mid purple
= = 374 Deep ochre

Backstitch in one strand

——— 267 Mid hunter green
——— 352 Very dark mahogany
——— 101 Mid purple

☆   Middle point

fabric

*wadding
(batting)*

*tape
measure*

*stranded
cotton*

scissors

*fabric-marker
pen*

needle

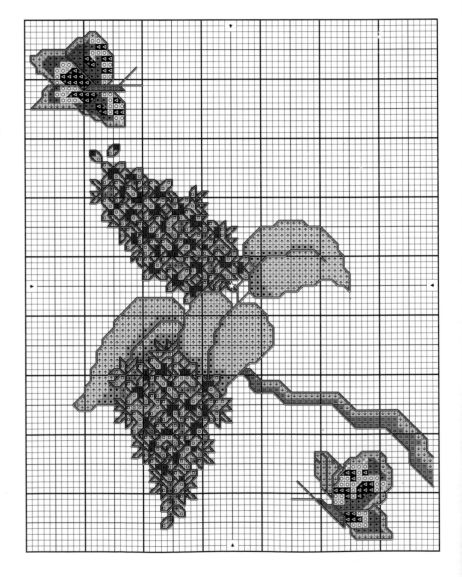

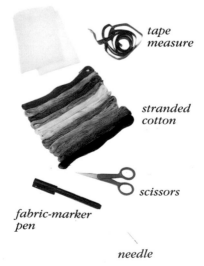

Lavender bag

Freshen up your wardrobe by hanging a sweet-smelling lavender bag. The distinctive scent will remind you of long refreshing walks and summers past.

1 Work the cross stitch in two strands throughout.

2 Backstitch the detail shown on the chart, using one strand of black.

YOU WILL NEED
Design size: 41 x 52
fabric: 14 hpi Aida, 15 x 16 cm
   (6 x 6¼ in)
26 tapestry needle
stranded cotton, as listed in key
tape measure
pins
sharp needle
sewing thread
scissors
large darning needle
46 cm (18 in) lavender ribbon,
   5 mm (¼ in) wide
dried lavender

Cross stitch in
two strands

✳✳	403 Black
··	1 White
⊐⊐	386 Cream
�H H	218 Deep green
●●	216 Light green
◁◁	117 Light mauve
○○	118 Mid mauve
►►	397 Pale grey

Backstitch in
one strand
——— 403 Black

☆   Middle point

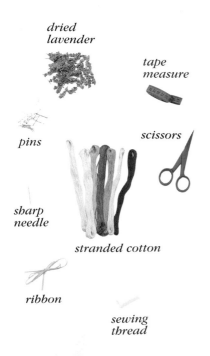

dried lavender

tape measure

pins

scissors

sharp needle

stranded cotton

ribbon

sewing thread

fabric

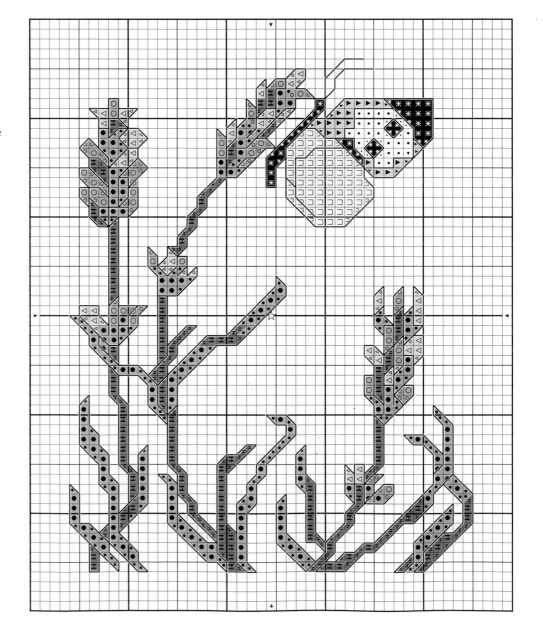

MAKING-UP INSTRUCTIONS

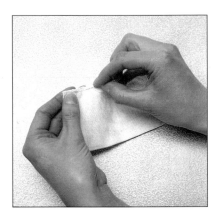

1 Fold under 1 cm (½ in) at the top of the work. Stitch to secure. With longer sides together, fold work in half, right sides enclosed, and stitch along this seam leaving a 1cm (½ in) edge.

2 Stitch a 1 cm (½ in) seam across the bottom of the bag. Turn to the right side and press. Taking a small pair of scissors, lightly snip vertically into the casing by the seam at the top of the bag at 1 cm (½ in) intervals. This is to form the ribbon casing.

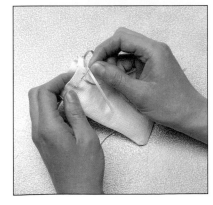

3 Thread the ribbon through the casing, using a large darning needle. Fill the bag with dried lavender and pull the ribbon to gather up the top. Tie in a bow to finish.

Frogs on waterlilies tray cloth

Create a tea-time treat and add a touch of humour to an afternoon snack with this whimsical tray cloth.

1 Starting from the centre, work the design using two strands for cross stitch and one for backstitch and French knots.

2 Lift the insert out of the middle of the tray.

3 Cut a piece of backing fabric the same size as the embroidered piece.

4 Put the backing fabric into the tray, followed by the embroidery and, finally, the insert.

YOU WILL NEED

Design size: 118 x 80
fabric: 14 hpi Aida, two pieces,
   18 x 25 cm (7 x 10 in)
26 tapestry needle
stranded cotton, as listed in key
mini craft tray 18 x 25 cm (7 x 10 in)
scissors

stranded cotton

26 tapestry needle

scissors

pencil

fabric

mini craft tray

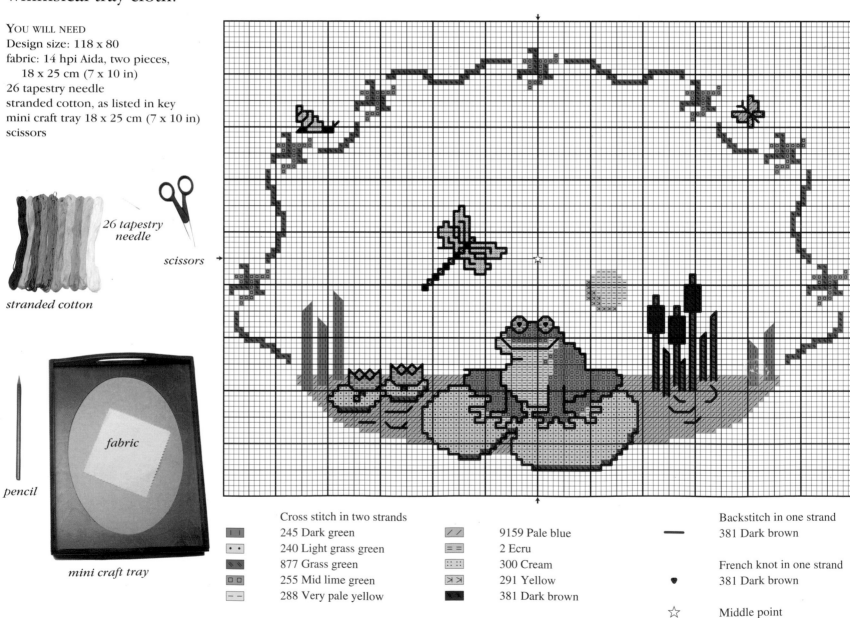

Cross stitch in two strands

I I	245	Dark green
· ·	240	Light grass green
◪ ◪	877	Grass green
□ □	255	Mid lime green
– –	288	Very pale yellow
⁄ ⁄	9159	Pale blue
= =	2	Ecru
⁚⁚ ⁚⁚	300	Cream
⋗ ⋗	291	Yellow
◼ ◼	381	Dark brown

Backstitch in one strand

— 381 Dark brown

French knot in one strand

● 381 Dark brown

☆ Middle point

Golden pheasant cabinet

Making a regal stance in the centre of this elegant cabinet, the golden pheasant will take pride of place in your home.

YOU WILL NEED

Design size: 45 x 45

fabric: 28 hpi evenweave over two threads, 15 x 15 cm (6 x 6 in)

26 tapestry needle

stranded cotton, as listed in key

craft display cabinet

cardboard

pencil

scissors

wadding (batting)

double-sided tape

1 Starting from the centre, work the cross stitch in two strands and the backstitch in one or two strands.

2 Cut a piece of cardboard to fit the centre section of the cabinet.

3 Place the embroidered piece face down on a flat surface and cut a piece of wadding (batting) the same size. Centre it over the embroidery and place the cardboard on top.

4 Attach double-sided tape around the edges of the cardboard and fold the edges of the fabric over to fix them on to the tape. Position the embroidery in the centre section of the cabinet.

scissors

fabric

stranded cotton

double-sided tape

craft display cabinet

wadding (batting)

26 tapestry needle

pencil

Cross stitch in two strands

▲ ▲	254 Dark yellow-green
◣ ◪	133 Blue
↑ ↑	305 Light gold
▪ ▪	308 Dark gold
■	403 Black
▬	1005 Dark red
I I	885 Cream
▽ ▽	259 Light green
▪ ▪	47 Light red
⊞ ⊞	227 Mid green
+ +	306 Mid gold

Backstitch in one strand

—— 403 Black

—— 268 Dark hunter green

Backstitch in two strands

—— 403 Black

French knot in one strand

⊘ 885 Cream

☆ Middle point

Dragonfly card

The beautiful, iridescent colours of the dragonfly are dramatically brought to life on this atmospheric card.

YOU WILL NEED
Design size: 35 x 43
fabric: 14 hpi Aida, 9 x 12 cm
   (3½ x 4½ in)
26 tapestry needle
stranded cotton, as listed in key
iron
towel
card with opening
pencil
wadding (batting)
scissors
double-sided tape

1 Starting from the centre of the design, work the dragonfly using two strands for cross stitch and one strand for backstitch.

2 When you have completed the design, check it for any marks. If it is grubby, you can rinse the stitching in warm, soapy water.

3 Allow it to dry flat and press lightly with the stitching face down on a towel so that you don't flatten the stitches.

4 Mount your work by following the instructions for filling a card.

26 tapestry needle

card with opening

stranded cotton

scissors

double-sided tape

wadding (batting)

fabric

pencil

Cross stitch in two strands

	217 Dark leaf green
	216 Mid leaf green
	215 Light leaf green
	Kreinik 094
	Kreinik 094 and Anchor 215 (one strand of each)
	210 Light blue green
	923 Mid blue green
	212 Dark blue green
	164 Deep turquoise
	170 Mid turquoise

Backstitch in one strand

	683 Dark green
	152 Dark blue

☆   Middle point

Honeysuckle café curtain border design

This creeping design covers the bottom of a curtain with panache and style.

YOU WILL NEED
Design size: 120 x 50 repeat design
fabric: 14 hpi Aida band, 10 x 87 cm
  (4 x 34 in)
24 tapestry needle
Marlitt thread, as listed in key
embroidery frame (optional)
scissors
1 m (39 in) cotton fabric
tape measure
pins
sharp needle
sewing thread
iron

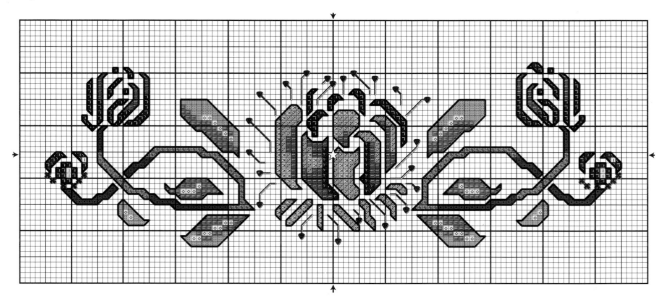

Aida band

Marlitt threads

embroidery frame

pins

cotton fabric

sewing thread

sharp needle

24 tapestry needle

scissors

tape measure

sewing thread

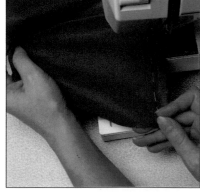

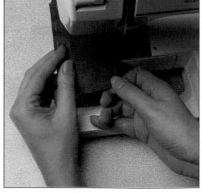

1 Work the design using two strands of Marlitt for cross stitch and one strand for backstitch and French knots. To make the curtain tabs, cut 16 pieces of cotton fabric, each one 10 x 26 cm (4 x 10 in). Position them in pairs with right sides facing. Pin, tack (baste) and machine stitch each pair together along three edges, leaving one short edge open. Turn right side out and press.

2 To make the curtain, turn under the side seams of the curtain by 2 cm (³/₄ in) twice and machine stitch.

3 Pin and tack (baste) a hem at the top and bottom of the curtain, then stitch the bottom hem. Fold the eight tabs in half and tack (baste) them in position evenly along the top edge of the curtain. Machine stitch the top hem, enclosing the tabs.

Cross stitch in two strands
Marlitt 895
Marlitt 1040
Marlitt 1039
Marlitt 894
Marlitt 881
Marlitt 852
Marlitt 897
Marlitt 1013
Marlitt 1212
Marlitt 893
Marlitt 1019

Backstitch in one strand
Marlitt 894
Marlitt 801

French knot in one strand
Marlitt 894

French knot in one strand
Marlitt 1072

☆ Middle point

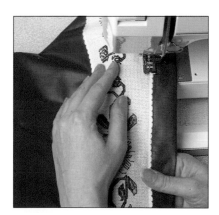

4 Attach the embroidered border. Place it directly above the bottom hem. Turn under the edges on the narrower sides and machine stitch to the curtain.

Lavender hat band

Brighten up a summer hat with a simple cross-stitch design. You can complete this lavender hat band in an evening.

YOU WILL NEED
Design size: 40 x 21 repeat
fabric: 5 cm (2 in) wide, 14 hpi Aida
    band, 1 m (1⅛ yd)
26 tapestry needle
stranded cotton, as listed in key
hat
tape measure
pins
scissors
sharp needle
sewing thread
iron

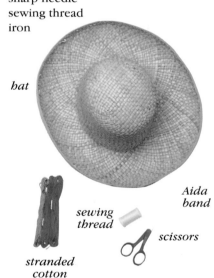

hat

stranded cotton

sewing thread

Aida band

scissors

pins

needle

26 tapestry needle

tape measure

MAKING-UP INSTRUCTIONS

1 Starting from the centre of the band, work the design using two strands for cross stitch and one strand for backstitch. Measure around the hat.

2 Use this measurement to find the centre point of the Aida band and mark it with a pin. Cut the band to size, leaving 1 cm (½ in) at each end for a seam. With right sides facing, backstitch along the seam. Press the seam open.

3 Pull the band over the hat, making sure the seam sits at the back of the hat.

Cross stitch in two strands
   112 Deep lavender
   98 Deep violet

Backstitch in one strand
— 263 Deep forest green

☆ Middle point

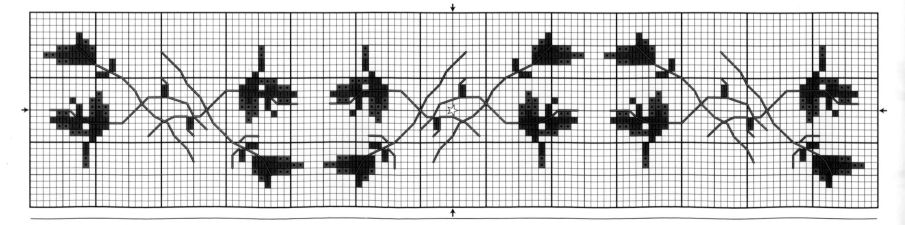

Corn-cob pot

Keep your Thanksgiving treats in this attractive harvest pot. And when you're done, use it to hold small change.

YOU WILL NEED

Design size: 42 x 36
fabric: 18 hpi Aida, 10 x 10 cm
(4 x 4 in)
26 tapestry needle
stranded cotton, as listed in key
iron
towel
7 cm (2½ in) craft pot
pencil
scissors
wadding (batting)

1 Starting from the centre of the design, work the cross stitch using two strands throughout.

2 When the work is complete, check it for marks. If it is grubby, you can rinse the stitching in warm, soapy water.

3 Allow it to dry flat and press lightly with the stitching face down on a towel so that you don't flatten the stitches.

4 Mount your work by following the instructions for filling a pot.

pot

stranded cotton

wadding (batting)

scissors

fabric

26 tapestry needle

pencil

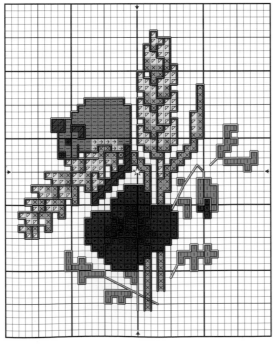

Cross stitch in two strands
▽ ▽	305 Light gold
■ ■	1006 Red
■ ■	46 Berry red
⊞ ⊞	382 Chocolate brown
◪ ◪	351 Mid mink
→ →	367 Cream
– –	1048 Mid peach
				229 Mid forest green
✕ ✕	306 Mid gold

Backstitch in two strands
——	382 Chocolate brown
——	229 Mid forest green
☆	Middle point

Wild rose card

Delight your mother on Mother's Day with this pretty floral card.

YOU WILL NEED
Design size: 94 x 60
fabric: 18 hpi Aida, 15 x 18 cm
   (6 x 7 in)
26 tapestry needle
stranded cotton, as listed in key
iron
towel
card with opening
pencil
wadding (batting)
scissors
double-sided tape

1 Starting from the centre of the design, work the motif using one strand of thread throughout.

2 When the work is complete, check it for marks. If it is grubby, you can rinse the stitching in warm, soapy water.

3 Allow it to dry flat and press lightly with the stitching face down on a towel so that you don't flatten the stitches.

4 Mount your work by following the instructions for filling a card.

card with opening

stranded cotton

fabric

wadding (batting)

26 tapestry needle

double-sided tape

scissors

pencil

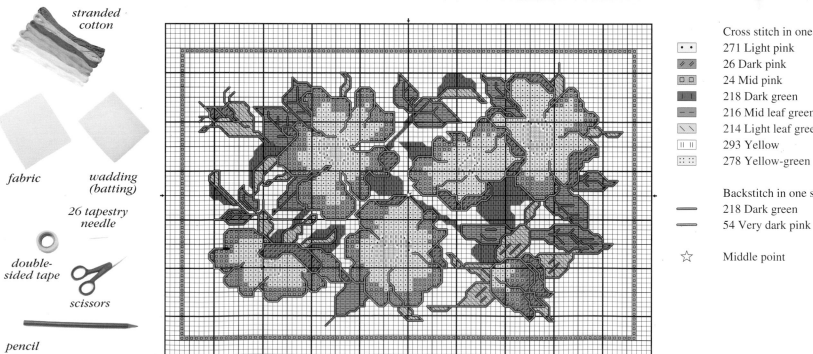

Cross stitch in one strand
271 Light pink
26 Dark pink
24 Mid pink
218 Dark green
216 Mid leaf green
214 Light leaf green
293 Yellow
278 Yellow-green

Backstitch in one strand
218 Dark green
54 Very dark pink

☆   Middle point

Butterfly shoulder-bag

Make yourself a unique shoulder-bag. This more challenging project uses beads, a variety of threads and a couple of different stitches.

MAKING-UP INSTRUCTIONS

1 Work the design using two strands of Marlitt thread for cross stitch and green French knots, and one strand for backstitch and black French knots. Use one strand of Kreinik throughout. Use sewing thread to attach the beads, working each stitch like a half cross stitch and threading on the bead before reinserting the thread into the fabric. Stitch the Aida and lining right sides together along the top and two sides.

YOU WILL NEED
Design size: 114 x 136
fabric: 14 hpi Aida, 30 x 71 cm
    (12 x 28 in)
24 tapestry needle
stranded cotton, as listed in key
Kreinik thread, as listed in key
Marlitt thread, as listed in key
embroidery frame
beading needle
small glass beads
cotton lining fabric, 1 m (39 in)
sewing thread
1 m (39 in) piping cord
sharp needle
7.5 cm (3 in) pieces of cardboard
pins
scissors
pencil

stranded
cotton

scissors

needles

sewing thread
pencil

card-
board   fabric

tape
measure

piping cord

lining

beads

pins
Kreinik
thread

embroidery
frame

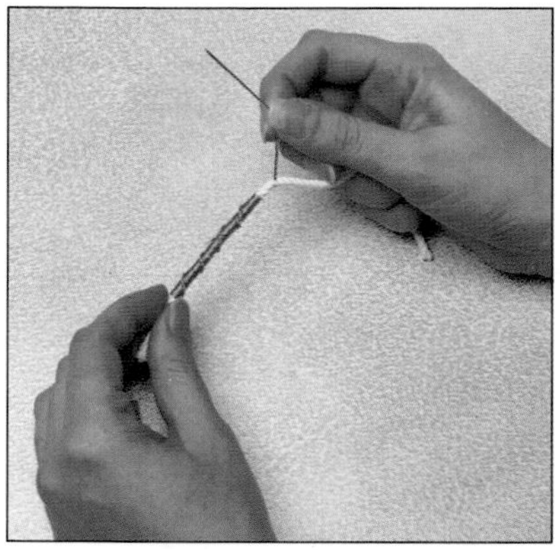

2 Make the bag strap by covering the piping cord with buttonhole stitch using four strands of Marlitt 858 and 863. Start buttonholing 2.5 cm (1 in) from the end of the cord.

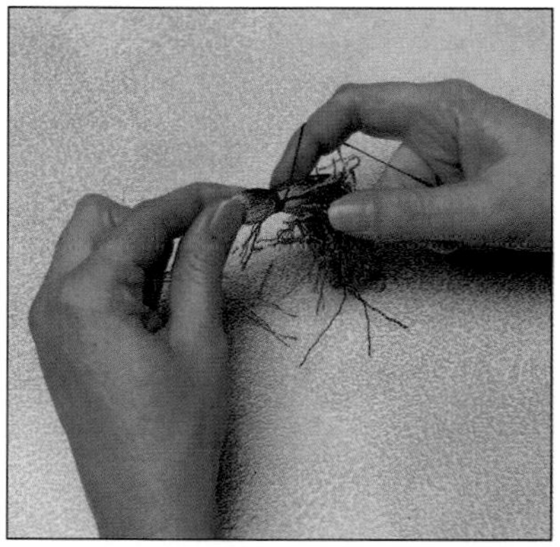

3 Make the tassels by wrapping thread around a 7.5 cm (3 in) piece of card. Slide a length of thread under the cardboard and pull tightly, drawing the threads together. Remove the threads from the cardboard. Wrap a 75 cm (30 in) length around the threads and finish by stitching into the tassel.

4 Turn the bag to the right side and fold it in half. Turn under 2.5 cm (1 in) at the top edge. Insert the cord and hold it in place with a few stitches.

5 Pin, tack (baste) and oversew the edges of the bag together. Attach two tassels at either side of the bag top.

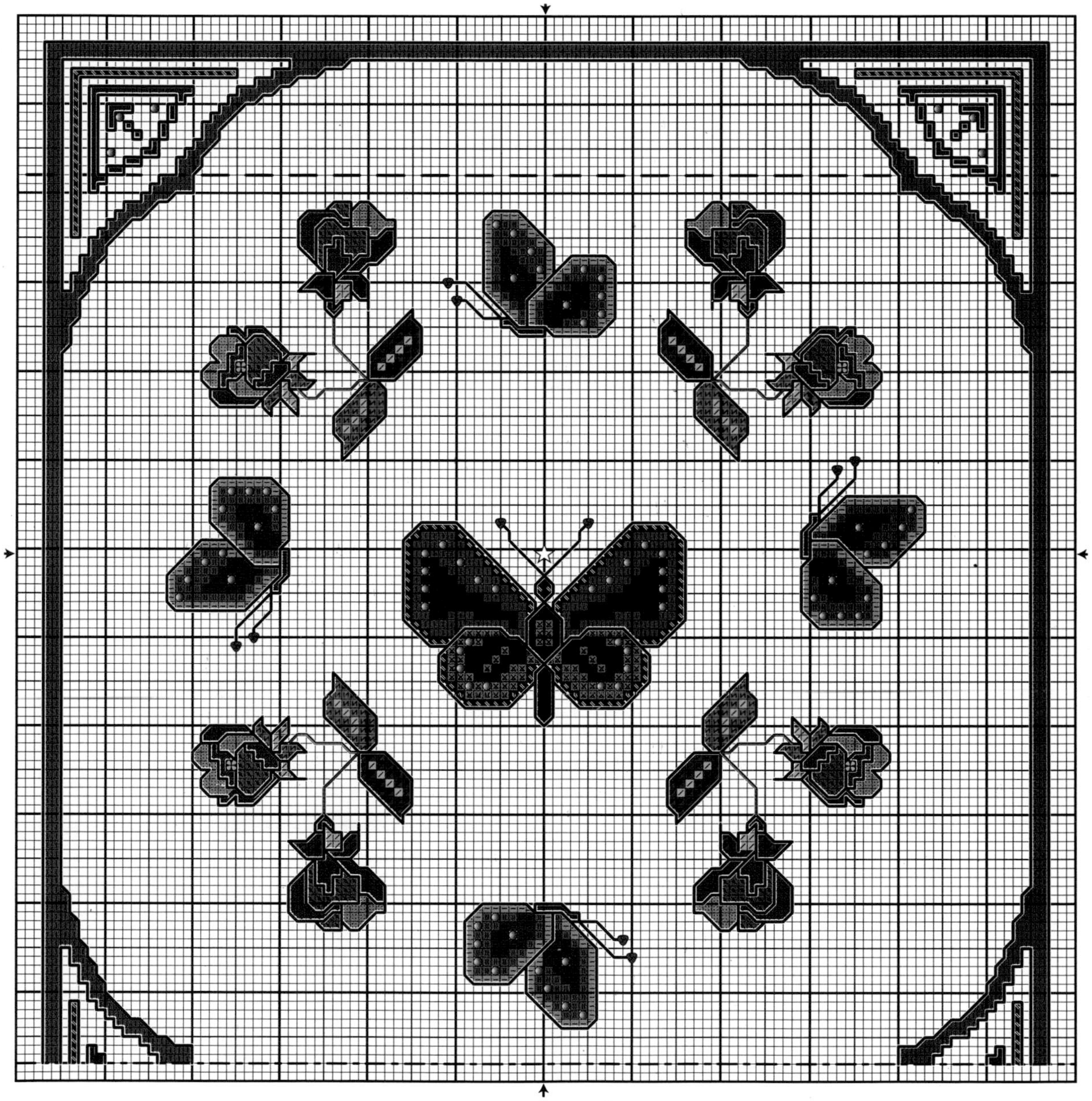

Cross stitch in one or two strands
- Marlitt 858 dark maroon
- Marlitt 863 maroon
- Kreinik fine braid 005 black
- Kreinik fine braid 001 light grey
- Marlitt 816 pearl grey
- Marlitt 817 light blue
- Marlitt 813 pale pink
- Marlitt 815 mid rose pink
- Marlitt 1069 dark rose pink
- Marlitt 853 green
- Marlitt 897 mint green
- Marlitt 852 blue green
- Marlitt 1072 brown
- Marlitt 859 purple
- Marlitt 857 light purple

Backstitch in one strand
- Marlitt 1072 brown
- Marlitt 801 black

Beading
- Mill Hill glass seed beads 00081

French knot in one strand
- Marlitt 801 black

French knot in one strand
- Marlitt 897 mint green

☆ Middle point

Oak tree hanging

The mighty oak is an emblem of constancy – strong and eternal. Create a symbolic hanging using this powerful subject.

YOU WILL NEED
Design size: 80 x 77
fabric: 28 hpi evenweave over two
    threads, 19 x 19 cm (7½ x 7½ in)
26 tapestry needle
stranded cotton, as listed in key
interfacing
iron
scissors
4 felt pieces, each 7.5 x 2.5 cm
    (3 x 1 in)
sharp needle
felt, 19 x 19 cm (7½ x 7½ in)
sewing thread
2 sticks, each 20 cm (8 in) long
cord with 2 tassels

	Cross stitch in two strands		Backstitch in one strand
■ ■	843 Dark green	——	236 Grey
⊞ ⊞	265 Very light hunter green	——	268 Dark hunter green
+ +	349 Brown		
▼ ▼	370 Mid mink	☆	Middle point
· ·	842 Light green		

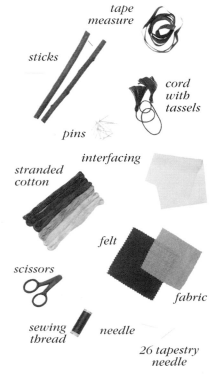

tape measure

sticks

cord with tassels

pins

interfacing

stranded cotton

felt

fabric

scissors

sewing thread

needle

26 tapestry needle

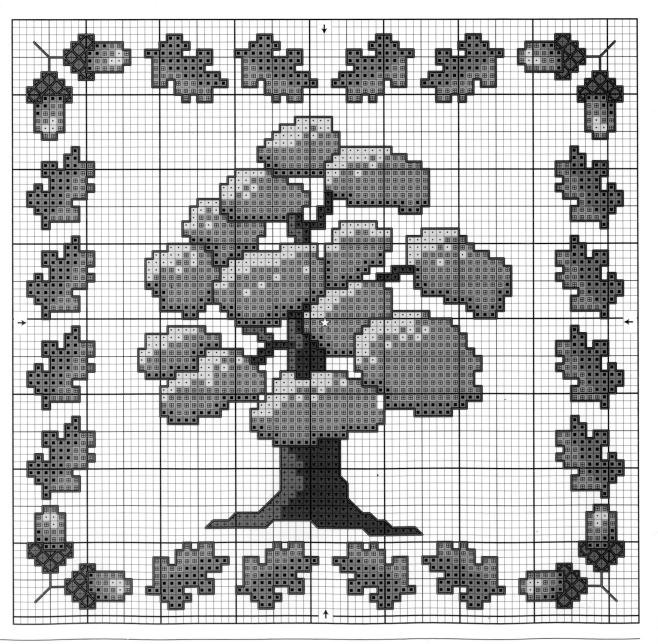

1 Starting from the centre of the design, work the motif using two strands for cross stitch and one strand for backstitch. Iron interfacing to the wrong side of the embroidered piece. Fold the pieces of felt in half across their width. Tack (baste) two felt tabs to the top of the embroidered piece and two to the bottom, approximately 2 cm ($^3/_4$ in) in from the corners.

2 With right sides of the large piece of felt and the evenweave facing, stitch around three sides, enclosing the tabs at the top and bottom edges.

3 Turn right side out and press. Slip stitch the side opening together and insert sticks through the felt tabs.

4 Attach a piece of cord, which has a tassel tied to each end, to the top stick and use to hang the finished work.

Foxglove mirror back

Pretty dressing-table sets have become popular
once again. Make a very special set using this
foxglove design.

YOU WILL NEED
Design size: 34 x 59
fabric: 28 hpi evenweave over two
    threads, 20 x 25 cm (8 x 10 in)
26 tapestry needle
stranded cotton, as listed in key
iron
interfacing
craft mirror back
pencil
scissors

Cross stitch in two strands
858 Light green
75 Clover pink
271 Light pink
859 Mid green
73 Pale pink

Backstitch in one strand
78 Very dark pink
862 Dark green

French knots in one strand
78 Very dark pink

☆ Middle point

stranded cotton

interfacing

mirror back

fabric

scissors

26 tapestry needle

pencil

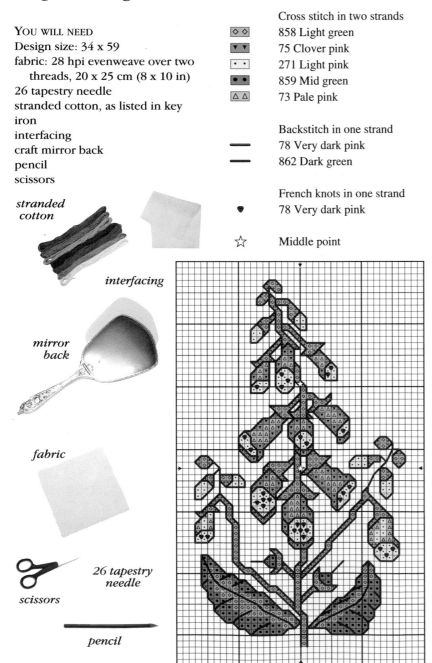

1 Starting from the centre of the
design, work the foxglove using two
strands for cross stitch and one strand
for backstitch and French knots.

2 Iron the interfacing on to the back of
the embroidery. When complete,
position the template supplied with the
mirror over the design and trace around
it. Cut neatly around the drawn line.

3 Take the mirror apart. Position the
embroidery against the metal frame plate
and insert the embroidery so that it faces
through the opening.

4 Reassemble the mirror.

Pig pot

People love pigs, especially cheeky ones. Surprise a friend by stitching them this charming pot. It'll make their day!

YOU WILL NEED
Design size: 36 x 25
fabric: 18 hpi Aida, 10 x 10 cm
   (4 x 4 in)
26 tapestry needle
stranded cotton, as listed in key
iron
towel
7 cm (2½ in) craft pot
pencil
wadding (batting)
scissors

1 Starting from the centre of the design, work the pig using two strands for cross stitch and one for backstitch and French knots.

2 When the work is complete, check for marks. If it is grubby, you can rinse the stitching in warm, soapy water.

3 Allow it to dry flat and press lightly with the stitching face down on a towel so that you don't flatten the stitches.

4 Mount your work by following the instructions for filling a pot.

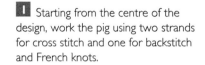
pot

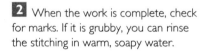

stranded cotton

scissors

fabric

wadding (batting)

26 tapestry needle

pencil

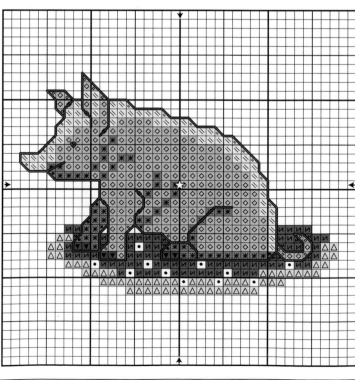

Cross stitch in two strands

✳✳	9575 Dark pink
▼▼	273 Grey
••	2 White
◣◣	1011 Light pink
и и	843 Dark green
◇◇	4146 Mid pink
△△	842 Light green

Backstitch in one strand
— 273 Grey

French knot in one strand
• 273 Grey

☆ Middle point

Summer meadow picture

Conjure up the the beauty of a summer's day with this picture that evokes all the warm, lazy, hazy days of summer.

1 Work the design using two strands for cross stitch and French knots, and one or two strands for backstitch.

2 When the work is complete, check it for marks. If it is grubby, you can rinse the stitching in warm, soapy water.

3 Allow it to dry flat and press lightly with the stitching face down on a towel so that you don't flatten the stitches.

4 Mount your work by following the instructions for lacing a picture.

YOU WILL NEED
Design size: 115 x 78
fabric: 14 hpi Aida, 30 x 20 cm
   (12 x 8 in)
26 tapestry needle
stranded cotton, as listed in key
iron
towel
ruler
pencil
cardboard
wadding (batting)
scissors
pins
sharp needle
sewing thread
picture frame

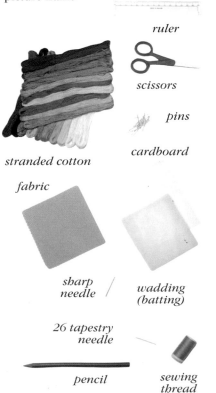

ruler

scissors

pins

cardboard

stranded cotton

fabric

sharp needle

wadding (batting)

26 tapestry needle

pencil

sewing thread

Cross stitch in two strands

| | | 1 White
| | 46 Berry
| | 47 Dark red
| ⌐⌐ | 73 Pale pink
| -- | 75 Clover pink
| ‖‖ | 130 Blue
| ⊏⊏ | 142 Dark blue
| ⋮⋮ | 245 Mid grass green
| ⋊⋉ | 279 Bright yellow
| ◇◇ | 280 Khaki green
| ↖↖ | 295 Cream
| ▽▽ | 298 Mid cream
| ╱╱ | 304 Apricot
| ╲╲ | 306 Pale apricot

| ⋈⋈ | 355 Mid cranberry
| ⋏⋏ | 357 Dark cranberry
| ⊠⊠ | 403 Black
| ✕✕ | 853 Mustard
| △△ | 855 Dark mustard
| ÷÷ | 858 Mint green
| ⊹⊹ | 875 Light forest green
| ++ | 877 Blue green
| ○○ | 887 Light khaki
| ⊥⊥ | 888 Mid sienna
| □□ | 900 Pearl grey
| ⊞⊞ | 924 Dark khaki
| ↓↓ | 943 Light brown

Cross stitch in mixed strands
(one of each colour)

| ←← | 295/275 Cream/pale cream
| ▽▽ | 280/275 Khaki green/pale cream
| ◙◙ | 280/924 Khaki green/dark khaki

Backstitch in one strand

| ——— | 858 Mint green
| —— | 403 Black

Backstitch in two strands

| —— | 357 Dark cranberry
| —— | 888 Mid sienna
| ≡≡ | 280 Khaki green
| —— | 877 Blue green

French knots in two strands

| ▽ | 275 Pale cream
| ▼ | 888 Mid sienna

| ☆ | Middle point

Buttercup cushion

If you hold a buttercup under your chin and your skin reflects the yellow, you are said to be good. Celebrate all things good by making this cushion and displaying it proudly in your home.

YOU WILL NEED
Design size: 120 x 120
fabric: 28 hpi evenweave over two
   threads, 30 x 30 cm (12 x 12 in)
26 tapestry needle
stranded cotton, as listed in key
pins
backing fabric
tape measure
30 cm (12 in) zip (zipper)
sharp needle
sewing thread
scissors
28 cm (11 in) cushion pad

Cross stitch in two strands
| | | 266 Light hunter green
| 268 Dark hunter green
| 298 Orange
| 292 Cream
| 289 Bright yellow
| 297 Mid yellow
| 306 Mid gold

269 Very dark hunter green
1 White
265 Very light hunter green

Backstitch in one strand
—— 269 Very dark hunter green

☆ Middle point

stranded cotton

sewing thread

pins

backing fabric

tape measure

fabric scissors

sharp needle

26 tapestry needle

zip (zipper)

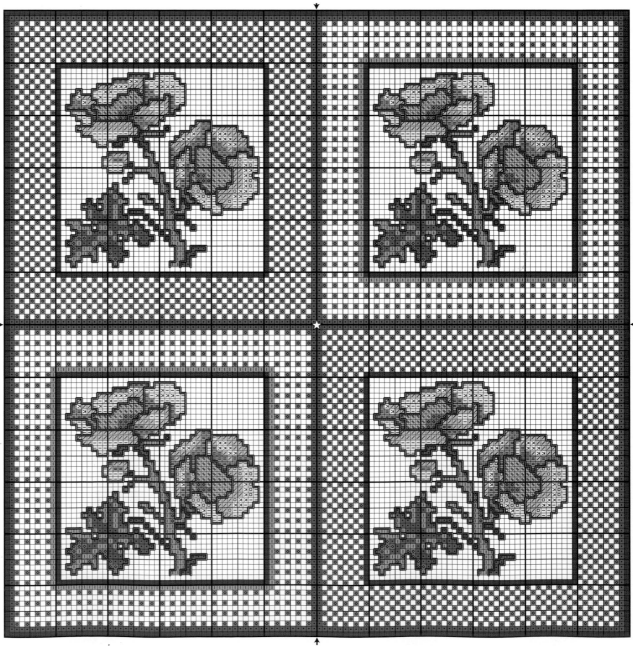

MAKING-UP INSTRUCTIONS

1 Work the design using two strands for cross stitch and one strand for backstitch. Lay the backing fabric over the embroidered piece with right sides facing. Stitch 1 cm (½ in) at either end of the top edge.

2 Insert the zip (zipper). With right sides facing you, place the zip (zipper) behind the fabric. Tack (baste) and stitch the zip (zipper) to the edge of the backing fabric. Then tack (baste) and stitch the front piece to the zip (zipper).

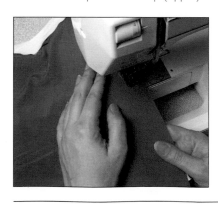

3 Open the zip (zipper) slightly. With right sides facing, stitch around the three open sides. Clip the corners.

4 Unzip the cushion cover and turn it to the right side. Fill the cushion with the cushion pad.

Strawberry paperweight

Lavish teas with fresh red strawberries epitomize all that is delicious about lazy, hazy, warm summer days. This strawberry paperweight keeps the memories fresh in your kitchen at all times.

YOU WILL NEED
Design size: 26 x 24
fabric: 14 hpi Aida, 13 x 13 cm
  (5 x 5 in)
26 tapestry needle
stranded cotton, as listed in key
craft paperweight
fabric-marker pen
scissors
glue

1 Work the cross stitch using three strands throughout.

2 Backstitch the detail on the chart, using one strand for each colour.

3 Use one strand of cream, wrapped 2–3 times around the needle, for random French knots on the strawberries for seeds.

4 Neatly finish off the work. Draw around the piece of felt supplied with the paperweight on to your design, centring the motif. Cut neatly around the drawn line. Place the embroidery under the paperweight and finish by gluing the felt on the bottom.

paperweight

glue

scissors

fabric-marker pen

fabric

26 tapestry needle

stranded cotton

Cross stitch in three strands
- ■ 9046 Bright red
- ⊡ 11 Coral red
- ⊡ 933 Cream
- ⊡ 243 Mid green
- ⊡ 264 Yellow green

Backstitch in one strand
— 72 Very deep garnet
— 246 Deep pine green

French knots in one strand
- ✆ 933 Cream

☆ Middle point

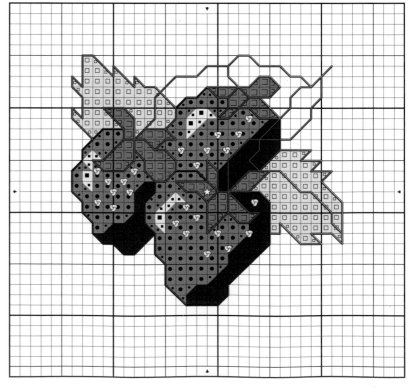

AUTUMN

Autumn leaves pot stand

With its large leaves and fruit, the horse chestnut makes a distinctive seasonal image. In an arrangement with oak leaves and acorns, it makes a perfect design for this pot stand.

YOU WILL NEED
Design size: 48 x 48
fabric: 28 hpi evenweave over
   two threads, 14.5 x 14.5cm
   (5½ x 5½in)
26 tapestry needle
stranded cotton, as listed in key
craft pot stand
tape measure
fabric-marker pen
scissors

1 Work the cross stitch in two strands throughout.

2 Backstitch the detail, using one strand for each colour.

3 Neatly finish off the work. Cut to the same size as the opening and place inside the pot stand. Secure with the backing card (cardboard) provided with the stand.

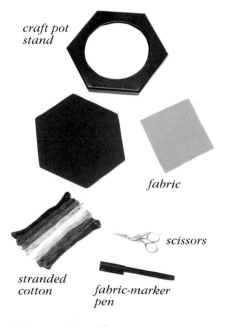

craft pot stand

fabric

scissors

stranded cotton

fabric-marker pen

26 tapestry needle

Cross stitch in two strands

⊐⊐	888 Deep mustard
‖ ‖	887 Mustard
■ +	352 Very dark mahogany
⬩⬩	349 Medium brown
÷ ÷	926 Off white
∧ ∧	369 Mid rust
И И	901 Very light brown
◇ ◇	842 Light green
⦙⦙⦙	845 Olive beige
▶ ▶	843 Dark sage green

Backstitch in one strand

— 846 Very dark avocado green
— 360 Brown

☆   Middle point

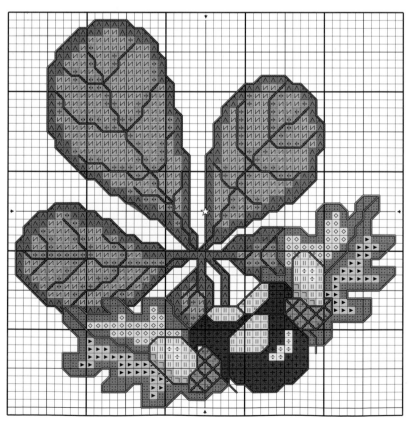

Autumn cushion

With the russets and browns of autumn beginning to appear, the colourful and distinctive blooms of this delightful cushion will provide a perfect memento of this time of year.

1 Work the cross stitch in two strands throughout.

2 Backstitch the details, using one strand for each colour.

3 Use one strand of yellow wrapped around the needle 2–3 times, for French knots in the centres of the purple flowers.

4 Neatly finish off the work and make up into your cushion following the instructions for the Spring cushion.

YOU WILL NEED
Design size: 136 x 138
fabric: 14 hpi Aida, 33 x 33 cm
  (13¼ x 13¼ in)
26 tapestry needle
stranded cotton, as listed in key
thimble
backing fabric
tape measure
fabric-marker pen
scissors
pins
sharp needle
sewing thread
cushion pad
lace trim

backing fabric

scissors

fabric-marker pen

26 tapestry needle

tape measure

stranded cotton

pins

thimble

Cross stitch in two strands
- – – 293 Pale yellow
- I I 241 Medium mint green
- + + 1043 Light mint green
- ✕ ✕ 261 Grass green
- ⋈ ⋈ 246 Deep pine green
- ∧ ∧ 48 Pale pink
- и и 50 Deep pink
- ◥ ◥ 41 Deep rose pink
- ╱ ╱ 75 Clover pink
- ⊁ ⊁ 267 Mid hunter green
- o o 265 Light green
- ⊤ ⊤ 852 Green grey
- ⊥ ⊥ 945 Deep cream
- = = 306 Mid gold
- ◁ ◁ 313 Light orange
- ▶ ▶ 304 Orange gold
- ⊟ ⊟ 316 Dull orange
- ⊓ ⊓ 256 Mid grass green
- ✶ ✶ 258 Dark yellow green
- ▲ ▲ 254 Mid green
- ● ● 387 Cream
- ■ ■ 334 Red orange
- ■ 47 Dark red
- → → 307 Gold
- ⊼ ⊼ 326 Rust orange
- △ △ 342 Pale mauve pink
- ◂ ◂ 109 Light violet

Backstitch in one strand
—— 879 Very dark blue grey
—— 877 Blue grass green
—— 23 Salmon pink
—— 1023 Dark pink
—— 944 Brown

French knots in one strand
⊕ 289 Yellow

☆ Middle point

Napkin and napkin ring

In these days of TV dinners and take-aways, it is so easy to forget the elegance of a formal dinner. This table linen, featuring a stylized tulip, could grace the most distinguished table.

YOU WILL NEED
Design size: 80 x 70
**fabric: linen napkin, 46 x 46 cm
   (18 x 18 in)**
ruler
sharp needle
tacking (basting) thread
stranded cotton, as used in key
iron
evenweave linen
26 tapestry needle

linen napkin

tacking (basting) thread

scissors

embroidery scissors

sewing cotton

needle

stranded cotton

NAPKIN

I Tack (baste) a guide line 4 cm (1½ in) in from the edge of one corner of the napkin. Work the cross stitch following the chart. The design uses single strands throughout except for the dark green thread on the "steps" at the bottom. Remove the tacking (basting) thread and press on the wrong side.

NAPKIN RING

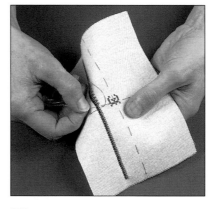

I Tack (baste) guide lines to mark the centre of the linen. Select the initial to be embroidered and work in cross stitch. Use two strands of mid pink cotton and work each stitch over two threads. Count 14 threads above the letter and work a row of cross stitch, measuring 13 cm (5 in), in dark green. Using mid pink, work another row of cross stitch underneath the first and a further row of single cross stitches below that. Leave two threads spaces between each row. On the next row, fill in these spaces with pale pink cross stitch. Work a last line of single cross stitch with two thread spaces in pink. Sew a similar border below the initial, reversing the order.

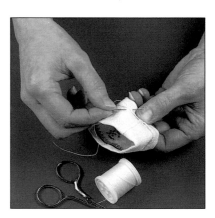

2 With right sides of the fabric together, join the two short edges to make a tube. Holding the seam open, turn up the top and bottom edges of the tube. Overlap these edges on the wrong side, so that only 5 mm (¼ in) of fabric shows above the cross stitch line on the right side. Slip stitch the edges together and turn the material through to the right side.

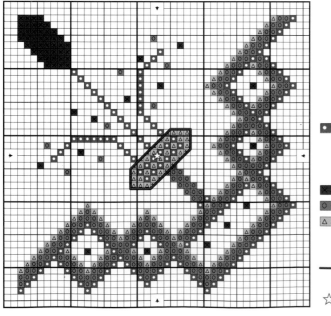

Cross stitch
in two strands
500 Dark green

Cross stitch
in one strand
915 Wine
3607 Mid pink
3609 Pale pink

Backstitch in one strand
915 Wine

☆ Middle point

Nesting squirrel pot

Saving his store of nuts for the winter, the squirrel hoards and stockpiles. This useful pot design celebrates his annual task. Why not stitch it for a friend so they can hoard their trinkets inside?

YOU WILL NEED
Design size: 40 x 37
fabric: 18 hpi Aida, 13 x 12 cm
 (5 x 4¾ in)
26 tapestry needle
stranded cotton, as listed in key
craft pot
fabric-marker pen
scissors
wadding (batting)

1 Cross stitch all four leaves using one strand, and two strands for the rest of the design.

2 Backstitch the detail using one strand of very dark mahogany throughout.

3 Neatly finish the work. Mount in a craft pot by following the instructions for filling a pot.

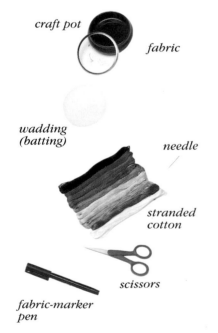

craft pot

fabric

*wadding
(batting)*

needle

*stranded
cotton*

scissors

*fabric-marker
pen*

Cross stitch in two strands

✳✳	845 Olive beige
O O	349 Medium brown
●●	842 Light green
↑↑	19 Deep red
↓↓	901 Very light brown
←←	362 Olive green
→→	1048 Light mahogany
◁◁	1 White
▶▶	360 Brown
ИИ	403 Black
⊓⊓	378 Light beige brown
⊐⊐	398 Pearl grey

Backstitch in one strand
—— 352 Very dark mahogany

☆ Middle point

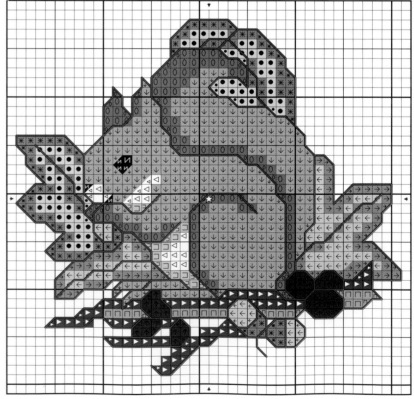

Halloween pumpkin

By late October children are preparing
for the excitement of Halloween. Fields of
pumpkins and boughs full of red and green
apples symbolize this time of year, and make a
perfect design for a special card.

YOU WILL NEED
Design size: 36 x 33
fabric: 28 hpi evenweave over two
threads, 14.5 x 13 cm
  (5½ x 5 in)
26 tapestry needle
stranded cotton, as listed in key
card with opening
wadding (batting)
fabric-marker pen
scissors
double-sided tape

1 Work the cross stitch in two
strands throughout.

2 Backstitch the detail, using one
strand for each colour.

3 Neatly finish off the design and
mount by following the instructions for
filling a card.

*card with
opening*

fabric

*wadding
(batting)*

scissors

*fabric-marker
pen*

*26 tapestry
needle*

stranded cotton

Cross stitch in two strands
✳✳	25 Rose pink
••	403 Black
I I	899 Light grey brown
+ +	898 Mid brown
■■	47 Dark red
⋉⋉	280 Olive
⋀⋀	889 Dark brown
И И	307 Gold
⋗⋗	306 Mid gold
⋮⋮⋮	358 Dark mink
••	267 Mid hunter green

Backstitch in one strand
— 403 Black
— 889 Dark brown
— 280 Olive
— 292 Cream
— 358 Dark gold brown

☆ Middle point

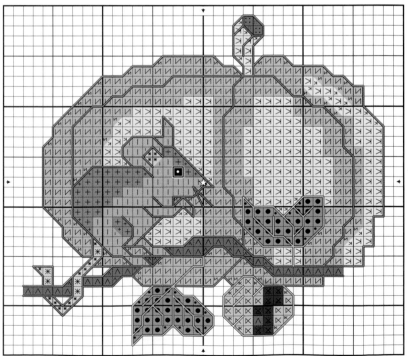

Harvest mouse

With fields of fresh wheat ready for harvest, the field mouse is a common sight on farms during the autumn months. Why not try this waste canvas project to enhance a T-shirt or baseball cap for a child?

YOU WILL NEED
Design size: 23 x 33
fabric: 14 hpi waste canvas,
  12 x 13 cm (4¾ x 5 in)
26 tapestry needle
stranded cotton, as listed in key
cotton T-shirt
sharp needle
sewing thread
scissors
cloth or sponge
water
tweezers

1 Work the cross stitch using two strands of stranded cotton throughout.

2 Backstitch the detail, using one strand for each colour.

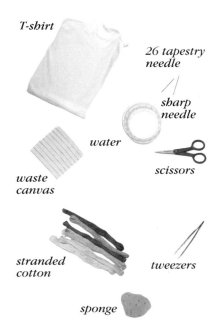

T-shirt

26 tapestry needle

sharp needle

water

scissors

waste canvas

stranded cotton

tweezers

sponge

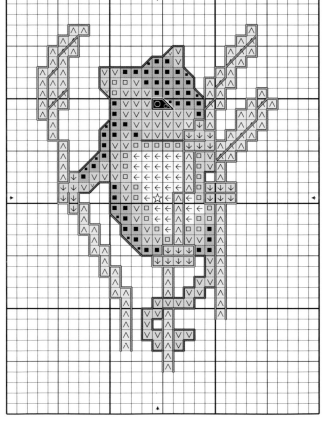

Cross stitch in two strands		Backstitch in one strand	
V V	362 Pale apricot	—	40 Deep pink
∧ ∧	288 Pale yellow	—	403 Black
← ←	926 Cream	—	351 Mid mink
↓ ↓	4146 Light peach flesh	—	914 Dark pink
■ ■	901 Tawny brown		
□ □	886 Beige		
● ●	403 Black	☆	Middle point

WORKING WASTE CANVAS

1 Tack (baste) the waste canvas to your garment where you want the design to be, and work your design.

2 Since the grid lines of the waste canvas are only a guide to positioning your stitches, extra care needs to be taken to keep your stitching even. The following hints might help:
a) Insert your needle in the centre of the waste canvas grid holes.
b) Make sure your stitches come up and go down in the same spot in the holes each time on your base material.
c) Start and finish off your threads very securely.
d) Do not stitch through the threads of the waste canvas – take particular care with fractional stitches.

3 When all the stitching is complete, remove tacking (basting) and trim away excess waste canvas. Take a clean wet cloth or sponge and dampen your work thoroughly.

4 Use tweezers to pull out each thread of waste canvas individually. If you have any difficulty at this stage, either you have not dissolved all the starch holding the waste canvas together or you have stitched through the canvas threads. In the former case, re-dampen your work and try again with the tweezers. If you have stitched through the waste canvas, you will need to cut the canvas either side of the trapped thread – be careful not to cut any of the cross stitching.

Autumn cottage

Falling leaves and brisk, fresh winds tell us that autumn is here. This picturesque little cottage weathers the elements as it stands guard and experiences the changing climate.

YOU WILL NEED

Design size: 106 x 76
fabric: 30 hpi linen over two
   threads, 26 x 20 cm
   (10¼ x 8 in)
26 tapestry needle
stranded cotton, as listed in key
picture frame
cardboard
tape measure
fabric-marker pen
scissors
wadding (batting)
pins
sharp needle
sewing thread

fabric

stranded cotton

scissors

tape measure

fabric-marker pen

needle

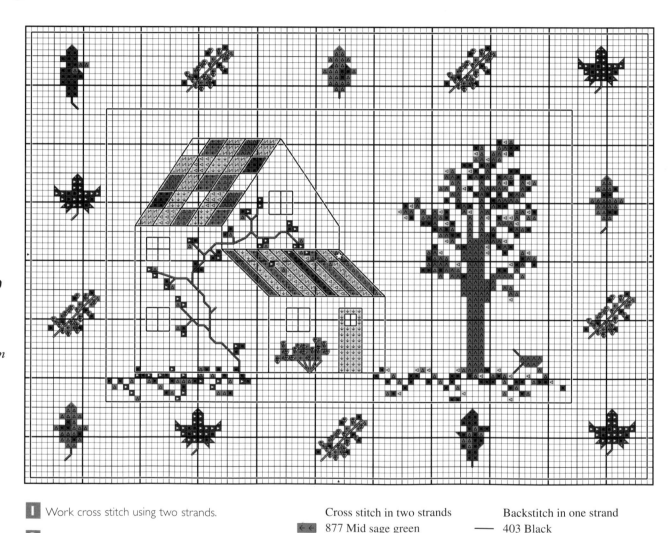

1 Work cross stitch using two strands.

2 Backstitch the detail following the chart for colours and using one strand throughout.

3 Neatly finish off your work, and mount it by following the instructions for lacing a frame.

Cross stitch in two strands

- 877 Mid sage green
- 976 Pastel blue
- 341 Deep rust
- 884 Dark blush
- 360 Brown
- 881 Flesh
- 891 Light gold
- 72 Very dark garnet

Backstitch in one strand

- —— 403 Black
- —— 381 Dark brown
- —— 360 Brown
- —— 341 Deep rust

French knots in one strand

- 341/884 Deep rust/dark blush
- ☆ Middle point

Doves in cote card

Delicate pastel shades make this card calm and gentle. The doves represent peace, so giving this card is a true sign of friendship.

YOU WILL NEED
Design size: 42 x 70
fabric: 14 hpi Aida, 10 cm x 15 cm
(4 x 6 in)
26 tapestry needle
stranded cotton, as listed in key
iron
towel
card with opening
pencil
wadding (batting)
scissors
double-sided tape

Cross stitch in two strands
27 Deep rose pink
23 Pink
1048 Mid rust
276 Deep cream
9159 Pale blue
206 Sea green
293 Yellow
235 Slate grey
234 Pearl grey
275 Pale cream

Backstitch in one strand
235 Slate grey

☆ Middle point

card with opening

fabric

wadding (batting)

double-sided tape

26 tapestry needle

scissors

stranded cotton

pencil

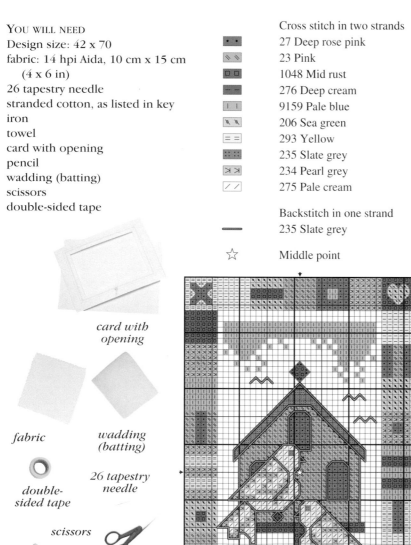

1 Starting from the centre of the design, work the motif using two strands for cross stitch and one for backstitch.

2 When the work is complete, check it for marks. If it is grubby, you can rinse the stitching in warm, soapy water.

3 Allow it to dry flat and press lightly with the stitching face down on a towel so that you don't flatten the stitches.

4 Mount your work by following the instructions for filling a card.

Fox pot

The fox has a mixed reputation – sly and sneaky or clever and endearing. Whatever your viewpoint, this fox design is an attractive project for all nature lovers.

YOU WILL NEED
Design size: 34 x 42
fabric: 18 hpi Aida, 15 x 15 cm
   (6 x 6 in)
26 tapestry needle
stranded cotton, as listed in key
iron
towel
8 cm (3 in) craft pot
pencil
scissors
wadding (batting)

1 Starting from the centre of the design, work the fox using two strands for cross stitch, one strand for the background trees and one for backstitch.

2 When the work is complete, check it for marks. If it is grubby, you can rinse the stitching in warm, soapy water.

3 Allow it to dry flat and press lightly with the stitching face down on a towel so that you don't flatten the stitches.

4 Mount your work by following the instructions for filling a pot.

pot

26 tapestry needle

stranded cotton

scissors

fabric

wadding (batting)

pencil

Cross stitch in two strands
403 Black
842 Light green
886 Dark cream
926 Cream
347 Light rust
349 Brown
351 Mid mink
843 Dark green

Cross stitch in one strand
379 Mid beige
376 Light beige

Backstitch in one strand
1050 Dark brown

☆   Middle point

Deer and fawn picture

In the forest the deer grazes with its fawn by its side. Mother and baby peek out from the safety of their woodland home.

1 Work your design using two strands for cross stitch and backstitch, and one for half cross stitch and French knots.

2 When the work is complete, check it for marks. If it is grubby, you can rinse the stitching in warm, soapy water.

3 Allow it to dry flat and press lightly with the stitching face down on a towel so that you don't flatten the stitches.

4 Mount your work by following the instructions for lacing a picture.

YOU WILL NEED
Design size: 120 x 113
fabric: 14 hpi natural Aida,
   30 x 28 cm (12 x 11 in)
26 tapestry needle
stranded cotton, as listed in key
iron
towel
ruler
pencil
cardboard
wadding (batting)
scissors
pins
sharp needle
sewing thread
picture frame

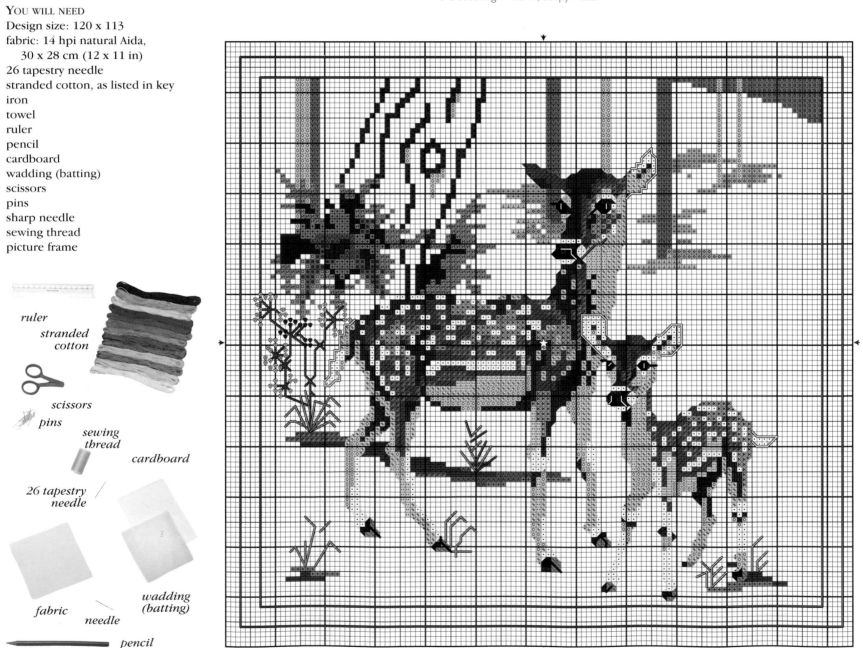

ruler

stranded cotton

scissors

pins

sewing thread

cardboard

26 tapestry needle

fabric

needle

wadding (batting)

pencil

Cross stitch in two strands

· ·	275 Pale cream
◊ ◊	276 Cream
+ +	308 Dark gold
▬ ▬	310 Mid brown
▬ ▬	351 Mid mink
·· ··	361 Light brown
▬ ▬	363 Mid tan
■ ■	403 Black
O O	831 Dark cream
⊥ ⊥	874 Light sage green
▢ ▢	887 Light forest green
⊞ ⊞	888 Mid sienna
▬ ▬	889 Dark brown
◈ ◈	898 Dark forest brown
◇ ◇	907 Mid brown
◣ ◣	1041 Very dark brown
◿ ◿	1048 Mid rust
◢ ◢	1049 Rust
＼ ＼	8581 Slate grey

Cross stitch in mixed strands
   (one of each colour)

и и	361/363 Light brown/mid tan
ʌ ʌ	308/310 Dark gold/mid brown
κ κ	363/1049 Mid tan/rust
Y Y	898/831 Dark forest brown/ dark cream

Half cross stitch in one strand
   (background)

S S	850 Slate blue
÷ ÷	907 Mid forest green

Backstitch in two strands

——	310 Mid brown
══	831 Dark cream
══	888 Mid sienna
——	1049 Rust
——	403 Black
══	1 White

French knots in one strand

●	363 Mid tan
✇	306 Mid gold

☆   Middle point

Cyclamen footstool cover

Footstools provide the opportunity for creating a wide range of cross-stitch designs. This cyclamen design is relatively easy to stitch and would make a good project for a beginner to try.

Cross stitch in two strands

- 87 Dark pink
- 214 Light green
- 217 Dark leaf green
- 215 Light leaf green
- 85 Light pink
- 86 Mid pink

Backstitch in one strand

— 879 Very dark forest green
— 1029 Very dark pink

☆ Middle point

YOU WILL NEED
Design size: 110 x110
fabric: 14 hpi Aida, 36 x 36 cm
   (14 x 14 in)
26 tapestry needle
stranded cotton, as listed in key
pencil
tape measure
scissors
sharp needle
sewing thread
28 cm (11 in) craft footstool
screwdriver

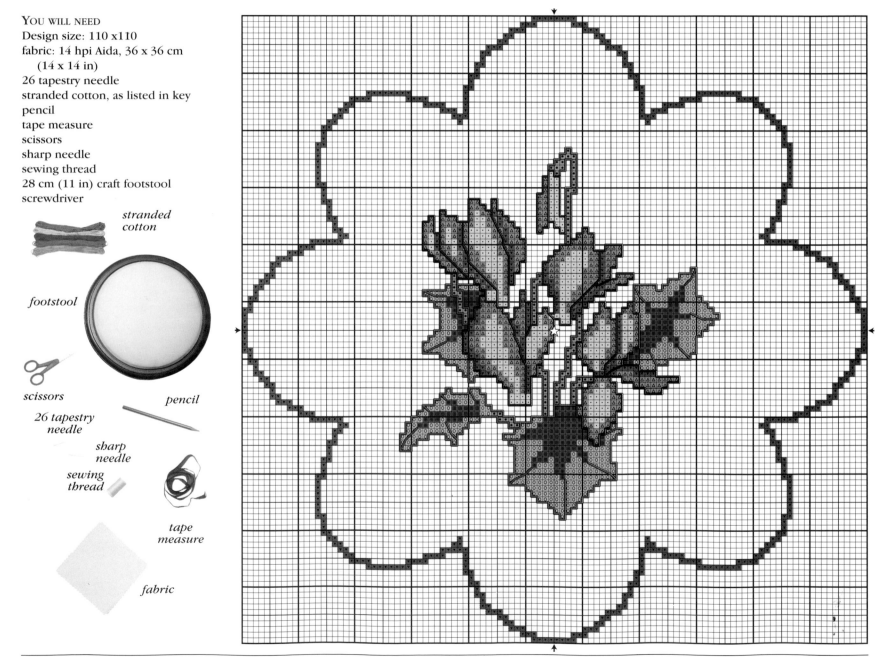

stranded cotton

footstool

scissors

pencil

26 tapestry needle

sharp needle

sewing thread

tape measure

fabric

MAKING-UP INSTRUCTIONS

1 Work the design using two strands for cross stitch and one for backstitch. When complete, draw a 36 cm (14 in) circle around it and cut it out.

2 Run a double gathering stitch 6 mm (¹/₄ in) inside the raw edge of the fabric.

3 Remove the pad from the footstool and place the design face up on the pad. Pull the gathering threads, adjusting the design as you go so that it remains in the centre of the stool.

4 Using a screwdriver, fix the base back on to the stool.

Squirrel paperweight

Furry woodland creatures such as squirrels make good cross-stitch designs and people enjoy receiving them.

YOU WILL NEED
Design size: 35 x 34
fabric: 18 hpi Aida, 10 x 10 cm
    (4 x 4 in)
26 tapestry needle
stranded cotton, as listed in key
8 cm (3 in) craft paperweight
pencil
scissors

1 First work the design using one strand throughout.

2 When complete, draw around the piece of felt supplied with the paperweight on to your design, centring the motif.

3 Cut neatly around the drawn line on the design.

4 Place the embroidery under the paperweight with the design facing into the glass and finish by placing the sticky felt on the bottom.

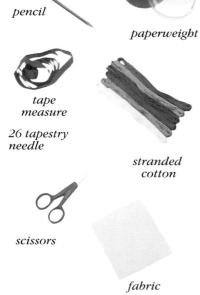

pencil

paperweight

tape measure

26 tapestry needle

stranded cotton

scissors

fabric

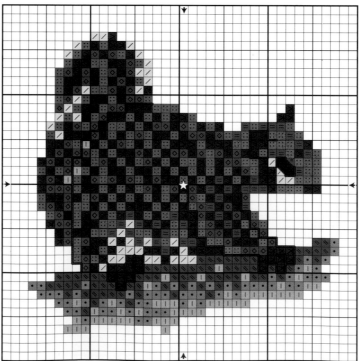

Cross stitch in one strand
273 Mid grey brown
8581 Stone grey
845 Sage
382 Chocolate brown
390 Cream
355 Claret brown
400 Slate grey
905 Mink brown
1041 Deep slate grey

Backstitch in one strand
— 905 Mink brown

☆ Middle point

TIP
If you wrap the edges of your fabric before stitching, with either masking tape or a zigzag stitch, it will prevent the fabric snagging or fraying while you are stitching it.

Mushrooms in basket card

This motif could also be used to decorate an apron or recipe box. It is a colourful kitchen design that looks great on a greetings card.

YOU WILL NEED
Design size: 43 x 60
fabric: 14 hpi Aida plus, 10 x 13 cm
    (4 x 5 in)
26 tapestry needle
stranded cotton, as listed in key
iron
towel
card with opening
pencil
wadding (batting)
scissors
double-sided tape

1 Starting from the centre of the design, work the motif using two strands for cross stitch and one strand for backstitch.

2 When the work is complete, check it for marks. If it is grubby, you can rinse the stitching in warm, soapy water.

3 Allow it to dry flat and press lightly with the stitching face down on a towel so that you don't flatten the stitches.

4 Mount your work by following the instructions for filling a card.

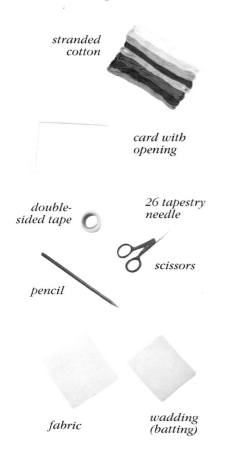

stranded cotton

card with opening

double-sided tape

26 tapestry needle

scissors

pencil

fabric

wadding (batting)

Cross stitch in two strands

ꞮꞮ	1 White
••	306 Mid gold
⑊⑊	886 Beige
→→	889 Dark brown
⫽⫽	214 Light green
▬▬	218 Dark green
▓▓	19 Claret red

Backstitch in one strand
— 236 Dark grey

☆ Middle point

Swan purse

Keep your pennies safe in this useful purse. Easy
to stitch and easy to make up, it's a design anyone
could try successfully.

YOU WILL NEED
Design size: 70 x 62
fabric: 14 hpi Aida, 15 x 15 cm
  (6 x 6 in)
26 tapestry needle
stranded cotton, as listed in key
backing fabric
tape measure
sewing thread
sharp needle
pins
10 cm (4 in) zip (zipper)
scissors

scissors

stranded
cotton

needle

backing
fabric

26 tapestry
needle

pins

sewing
thread

tape
measure

zip
(zipper)

fabric

Cross stitch in two strands		Backstitch in one strand
1 White	215 Light leaf green	—— 403 Black
403 Black	214 Light green	
397 Pearl grey	74 Clover pink	☆ Middle point
127 Royal blue	301 Lemon yellow	
979 Navy blue	176 Mid sky blue	
218 Dark green	128 Sky blue	

MAKING-UP INSTRUCTIONS

1 Work the design using two strands for cross stitch and one strand for backstitch. Lay the backing fabric over the embroidered fabric with right sides facing. Stitch 1 cm (½ in) at either end of the top edge.

2 Insert the zip (zipper). With right sides facing you, place the zip (zipper) behind the fabric. Tack (baste) and stitch the zip (zipper) to the edge of the backing fabric. Then tack (baste) and stitch the front piece to the zip (zipper).

3 Open the zip (zipper) slightly. With right sides facing, stitch around the three open sides.

4 Clip the corners and turn the purse right side out.

Owl apron

Cheer up a plain apron by stitching a quirky design on to the front. This cheeky owl is great fun to stitch.

YOU WILL NEED
Design size: 56 x 55
fabric: 14 hpi Aida, 13 x 13 cm
    (5 x 5 in)
26 tapestry needle
stranded cotton, as listed in key
sharp needle
apron
scissors
sewing thread
pins

apron

stranded cotton

tape measure

sewing thread

pins

26 tapestry needle

needle

fabric

scissors

Cross stitch in two strands

∴	350 Deep pink
◊◊	3340 Deep apricot
⌐⌐	725 Mid beige
‖‖	906 Bright green
═	830 Dark brown
⠿	677 Cream
▷▷	729 Dark cream
◤◣	300 Reddish-brown
▽▽	415 Pearl grey
▮▮	310 Black
∕∕	001 White

Backstitch in one strand

— 310 Black
— 986 Dark forest green
— 840 Mid brown

French knot in two strands

✱ 403 Black

☆ Middle point

MAKING-UP INSTRUCTIONS

1 Work the design using two strands for cross stitch and French knots, and one strand for backstitch. Turn under the edges of the design by about 1 cm (½ in) and tack (baste) them in place.

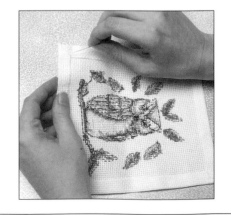

2 Position the design on the front of the apron.

3 Tack (baste) it on to the front of the apron front ready for stitching.

4 Sew around the design using a straight stitch. Alternatively, you could zigzag over the edges of the design. Trim away any loose threads.

Blackberry card

Do you remember autumn afternoons spent collecting delicious blackberries to make jelly? Stitch this card in memory of those nostalgic times.

YOU WILL NEED
Design size: 29 x 39
fabric: 18 hpi Aida, 13 x 12 cm
  (5 x 4¾ in)
26 tapestry needle
stranded cotton, as listed in key
card with opening
wadding (batting)
fabric-marker pen
scissors
double-sided tape

1 Work the blackberries and flowers using two strands of cross stitch. Use one strand for cross stitching the leaves.

2 Backstitch the detail, using one strand for each colour.

3 Neatly finish off the work and mount by following the instructions for filling a card.

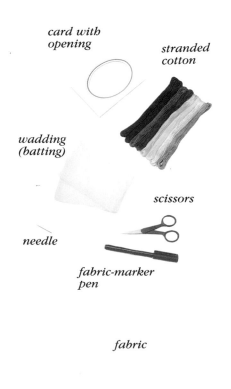

card with opening

stranded cotton

wadding (batting)

scissors

needle

fabric-marker pen

fabric

Cross stitch in two strands
- 65 Deep raspberry
- ∧ ∧ 24 Rose pink
- И И 872 Deep lilac
- + + 289 Yellow

Cross stitch in one strand
- ⊠ ⊠ 264 Yellow green
- ■ ■ 265 Light green

Backstitch in one strand
— 65 Deep raspberry
— 872 Deep lilac
— 403 Black
— 267 Mid hunter green

☆ Middle point

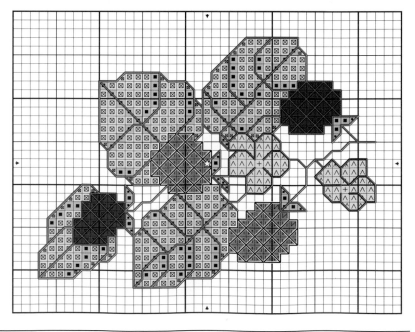

Apple and pear placemats

Cross stitch is so versatile, you can use it for almost anything. Creating a complete place setting can be satisfying and extremely attractive – use the same chart for each, picking out either the pear or the apple for the napkin holder.

YOU WILL NEED
Design size: 38 x 37
fabric: ivory 11 hpi Aida,
  36 x 30 cm (14 x 12 in)
ivory 11 hpi waste canvas,
  12.5 x 12.5 cm (5 x 5 in)
ivory 18 hpi Aida, approx.
  7.5 x 7.5 cm (3 x 3 in)
26 tapestry needle
thimble
stranded cotton, as listed in key
tape measure
fabric-marker pen
iron
scissors
iron-on interfacing
cream cotton backing fabric
pins
sharp needle
sewing thread
napkin
napkin holder

fabrics

napkin

napkin holder

fabric-marker pen

stranded cotton

thimble

tape measure

needle

scissors

FOR THE PLACEMAT

1 Position the design 4 cm (1½ in) up from the bottom edge of the fabric and 4 cm (1½ in) in from the left-hand edge. Use three strands throughout for the cross stitch.

2 Turn under the edges by 1.5 cm (⅝ in) all around, and iron flat. Cut a piece of medium-weight iron-on interfacing 33 x 30 cm (13¼ x 12 in) and iron on the reverse of the design, placing it between the turned edges

3 Take a piece of cream-coloured cotton backing fabric 36 x 30 cm (14 x 12 in), turn under a 1.5 cm (⅝ in) edge all around and press. Place on reverse of placemat with the turned edges sandwiched together; pin and slip stitch the backing to the placemat.

FOR THE NAPKIN

1 Tack (baste) the waste canvas to a corner of the napkin and stitch the design, using 3 strands throughout. Dampen and remove the waste canvas and tacking (basting) stitches.

FOR THE NAPKIN HOLDER

1 Stitch either the pear or the apple using one strand throughout. Trim Aida to approx 5 x 5 cm (2 x 2 in) and iron under edges all round to make the finished piece approximately 4 x 4 cm (1½ x 1½ in) to fit napkin holder. Insert into holder.

Cross stitch in three strands for placemat and napkin.
Cross stitch in one strand for napkin holder.

✳✳	215 Light leaf green
··	216 Light green
⊁⊁	886 Beige
OO	214 Leaf green
▼▼	277 Dark sage green
◁◁	887 Mustard
▶▶	268 Dark hunter green
ИИ	4146 Light peach flesh
▫▫	278 Very light avocado green
■■	265 Light green
∧∧	10 Coral red
⊐⊐	13 Christmas coral
⊓⊓	393 Very dark mushroom
♡♡	217 Mid leaf green
◇◇	903 Brown
☆	Middle point

Chicken tea cosy

Outside the farmhouse door the yard is full
of pecking hens, ducks and geese. Amid the
cackling din, the farmer's wife goes about her
daily chores. It's a lively scene with an air of
gentle tranquillity. And a challenging project for
even the most experienced stitcher.

YOU WILL NEED
Design size: 192 x 136
fabric: 14 hpi Aida, 42 x 32 cm
  (16½ x 13 in)
26 tapestry needle
stranded cotton, as listed in key
backing fabric
tape measure
scissors
pins
sharp needle
sewing thread
wadding (batting)

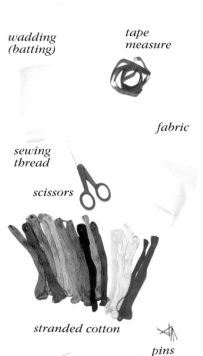

wadding (batting)

tape measure

fabric

sewing thread

scissors

stranded cotton

pins

needle

Cross stitch in two strands

I I	403 Black	/ /	398 Pearl grey	Q Q	851 Blue green
+ +	1 White	◊ ◊	397 Pale grey	← ←	924 Deep olive green
X X	380 Dark brown	⊃ ⊃	292 Light lemon	↓ ↓	212 Dark green
⋉ ⋉	371 Mid brown	o o	305 Light yellow beige	□ □	130 Blue
∧ ∧	351 Mink brown	↑ ↑	335 Vermillion	⊥ ⊥	6 Light salmon
и и	368 Mid beige	⋉ ⋉	46 Berry red		
⟍ ⟍	400 Slate grey	▲ ▲	47 Dark red		

Backstitch in one strand

—— 403 Black

☆ Middle point

MAKING-UP INSTRUCTIONS

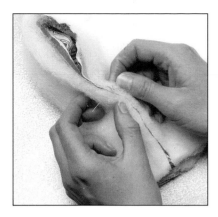

1 Work the cross stitch using two strands throughout. Backstitch the detail using one strand of black. Cut the design and backing fabric into a semi-circle, with the bottom of the design along the straight edge. Sew the design to the backing fabric with right sides together, leaving a 1.5 cm (⅝ in) seam.

2 Sew the lining together, along the semi-circle, leaving the bottom edge open. Attach the wadding (batting) by tacking (basting) the seam to the wrong side of the front and back of the cosy.

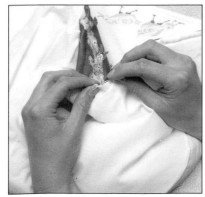

3 Attach the cosy to the lining, right sides together, leaving a gap of 1.5 cm (⅝ in) for turning.

4 Turn the cosy right sides out, and finish off the open edge with small invisible stitches.

Bees and honey tea towel

Add a little decorative detail to your kitchen
linen to grace your towel rail, by stitching this
original yet simple hive design.

YOU WILL NEED
Design size: 70 x 14
fabric: 14 hpi Aida tea towel
26 tapestry needle
stranded cotton, as listed in key
scissors

tea towel

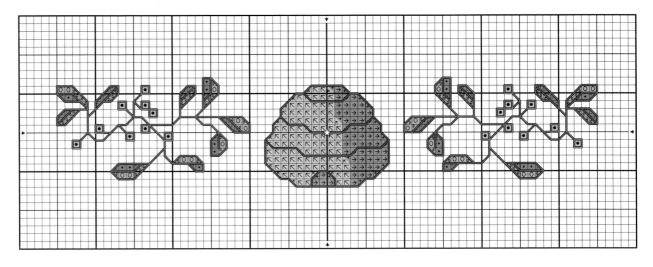

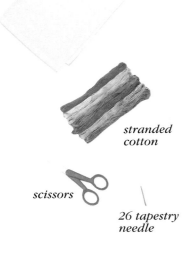

*stranded
cotton*

scissors

*26 tapestry
needle*

1 Work the cross stitch using two
strands throughout. Backstitch the detail
in the following colours: dark hunter
green for the leaf detail (two strands),
dark pink for the flowers (one strand)
and brown for the hive (two strands).

2 To stitch the work evenly on the
tea towel, start at the centre and stitch
a hive with floral detail on either side.

3 Leave 4 holes before working your
next repeat. Make sure you balance the
design by working the same element
on both the left and right sides of
the centre.

Cross stitch in two strands
- 267 Mid hunter green
- 280 Olive
- 23 Salmon pink
- 907 Golden brown
- 365 Dark golden brown

Backstitch in two strands
— 268 Dark hunter green
— 357 Brown

Backstitch in one strand
— 26 Dark pink

☆ Middle point

Autumn sampler

With animals preparing for the winter, autumn is a busy time in the country. This sampler is packed with country plants and creatures that can be seen regularly at this time of year.

YOU WILL NEED

Design size: 111 x 139
fabric: 28 hpi evenweave over
 two threads, 27 x 31 cm
 (10½ x 12¼ in)
26 tapestry needle
stranded cotton, as listed in key
picture frame
cardboard
fabric-marker pen
tape measure
scissors
wadding (batting)
pins
sharp needle
sewing thread

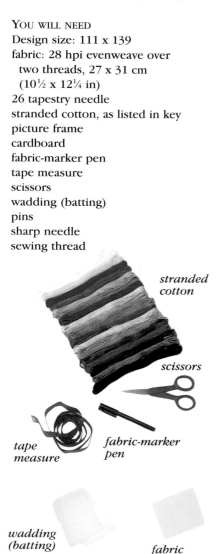

stranded cotton

scissors

tape measure

fabric-marker pen

wadding (batting)

fabric

needle

Cross stitch in
 two strands

⠒⠒	267 Mid hunter green
⊓⊓	264 Green yellow
━━	19 Deep red
Ⅰ Ⅰ	333 Scarlet
Ⅱ Ⅱ	146 Blue
∧∧	403 Black
÷ ÷	1 White
△△	290 Dark lemon
××	398 Pearl grey
∧∧	400 Slate grey
⁄⁄	24/259 Rose pink/ very light green
⧄⧄	19/259 Deep red/ very light green
▲▲	399/349 Mid grey/ mid brown
■■	399 Medium grey
↖↖	108 Lilac
◀◀	102 Dark purple
↓↓	1004 Rust brown
⊥⊥	382 Very dark brown
0 0	351 Mid mink
⠿⠿	349 Medium brown
▷▷	347 Fawn
◇◇	386 Cream
▽▽	259 Light green

☆ Middle point

For backstitch
colours, see Step 2
on facing page.

---

1 Work the cross stitch using two stands throughout.

2 Backstitch the details, using one strand, for each of the following colours. Blackberries: dark green for veins on leaves; dark purple for outline of blackberries; lilac for markings on berries; slate grey for outlining elsewhere. Tortoiseshell butterfly: black for internal markings and mid mink for outlines. Rosehips: dark green for veins on leaves; slate grey for outlines. Spider and spider's web: black for spider's legs and outline; white for spider's web. Harvest mouse: slate grey for whiskers and outlines. Goldfinch: slate grey for outlines; mid mink for branch. Crab apples: medium brown for bud marks on bottom of apples; slate grey for outline and dark green for veins on leaves. Pears: medium brown for bud marks, slate grey for outlines. Large white butterfly: slate grey for veins on lower wing; and outlines. Oak leaves: mid mink for veins on leaves; slate grey for outlines. Robin: mid mink for veins on leaves and markings on wings; slate grey for outlines. Hazelnuts: very dark brown for veins on leaves; slate grey for outlines. Squirrel: slate grey for outline; white French knot for squirrel's eye and pearl grey for long stitches sewn at random lengths following the shape of the tail. Funghi: white French knots at random and slate grey for outlines. Alphabet letters: use two strands of mid mink and also for outline of box.

3 Neatly finish off the work and lace it by following the instructions for lacing a frame.

Autumn scene

Recall the dazzling hues of a crisp autumnal day with this esoteric design.

YOU WILL NEED
Design size: 49 x 68
fabric: 14 hpi natural Aida,
    18 x 23 cm (7 x 9 in)
26 tapestry needle
stranded cotton, as listed in key
iron
towel
ruler
pencil
cardboard
wadding (batting)
scissors
pins
sharp needle
sewing thread
picture frame

1 Work the design using two strands for cross stitch and one for backstitch.

2 When the work is complete, check it for marks. If it is grubby, you can rinse the stitching in warm, soapy water.

3 Allow it to dry flat and press lightly with the stitching face down on a towel so that you don't flatten the stitches.

4 Mount your work by following the instructions for lacing a picture.

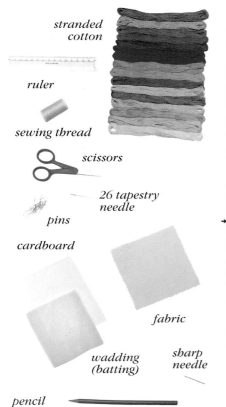

stranded cotton

ruler

sewing thread

scissors

26 tapestry needle

pins

cardboard

fabric

wadding (batting)

sharp needle

pencil

Cross stitch in two strands

I I	19 Claret red	И И	1014 Light berry red
• •	46 Berry red	∧ ∧	1047 Mid beige
⁓ ⁓	280 Mid grass green	✳ ✳	1048 Mid peach
→ →	298 Deep yellow	Y Y	5975 Deep russet
─ ─	349 Mid rust	S S	8581 Charcoal grey
✕ ✕	357 Deep rust	∓ ∓	977 Sky blue
= =	361 Yellow cream	⊞ ⊞	1024 Deep pink
⁞ ⁞	363 Mid tan		
⇥ ⇥	376 Light grey		
◇ ◇	379 Mid beige		**Backstitch in one strand**
⬩ ⬩	868 Light sienna	───	877 Grass green
▽ ▽	877 Grass green	───	889 Dark brown
╱ ╱	889 Dark brown	───	1014 Light berry red
╲ ╲	900 Mid grey	───	8581 Charcoal grey
		☆	Middle point

Pears table set

Make a complete set of napkins and napkin holders. The pear design is easy and quick to stitch and will add a unique touch to your table.

YOU WILL NEED

Design size: 20 x 21
fabric: 18 hpi Aida and 14 hpi waste canvas
26 tapestry needle
stranded cotton, as listed in key
craft napkin holder
napkin
sharp needle
sewing thread
scissors
tweezers (optional)

1 For the napkin holder, work the design on the Aida using one strand throughout. Insert the finished design into the napkin holder.

2 For the napkin, adapt the pear motif to make a new design, or simply use the same pattern as on the napkin holder. Tack (baste) a piece of waste canvas on to the napkin where you want the design to appear.

3 Work the design through both the napkin and the waste canvas using two strands for cross stitch and one strand for backstitch.

4 To remove the waste canvas, just lightly dampen your work. As the canvas softens, you can remove it thread by thread. This may be easier to do with a pair of tweezers.

napkin

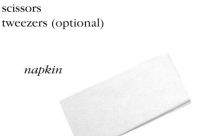

stranded cotton

craft napkin holder

fabric

scissors

26 tapestry needle

tape measure

pencil

sharp needle

sewing thread

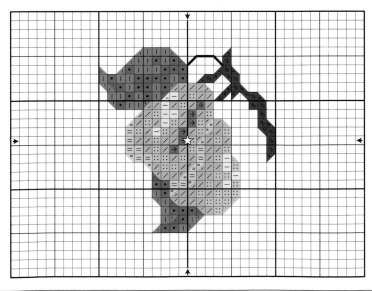

Cross stitch in one or two strands

	216 Mid leaf green
	217 Dark leaf green
	358 Dark mink
	895 Light red brown
	886 Creamy green
	945 Mid creamy green
	888 Mid sienna
	874 Apricot

Backstitch in one strand
— 403 Black

☆ Middle point

Robin needlecase

Stuck for ideas for Christmas presents? If so, why not make this practical and attractive needlecase? It's an easy project for a beginner and people love receiving handmade gifts.

YOU WILL NEED
Design size: 27 x 26
fabric: 28 hpi evenweave over two
    threads, four pieces 11 x 10 cm
    (4¹/₂ x 4 in)
26 tapestry needle
stranded cotton, as listed in key
iron
interfacing
tape measure
sharp needle
sewing thread
pins
felt
scissors

stranded cotton

interfacing

tape measure

26 tapestry needle

needle

scissors

sewing thread

fabric

pins

felt

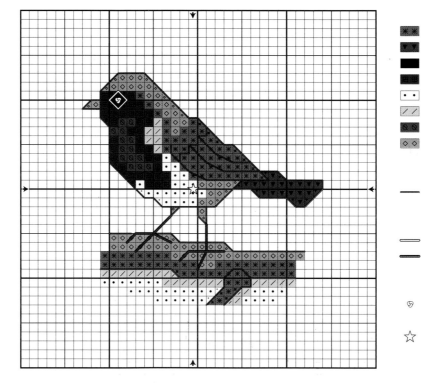

	Cross stitch in two strands
✱ ✱	349 Brown
▼ ▼	351 Mid mink
■	403 Black
▨	9046 Dark red
··	2 White
⁄⁄	234 Grey
⊗ ⊗	335 Light red
◇ ◇	347 Light brown

Backstitch in one strand
352 Very dark brown

Backstitch in two strands
2 White
352 Very dark brown

French knot in one strand
2 White

☆ Middle point

MAKING-UP INSTRUCTIONS

1 Work the design on one of the pieces of evenweave using two strands for cross stitch and some backstitch, and one strand for French knots and remaining backstitch. Iron interfacing to the back of the embroidered piece and one other piece of evenweave. Lay each piece with interfacing on one of the remaining evenweave pieces and, with right sides facing, stitch along two long edges and one short edge.

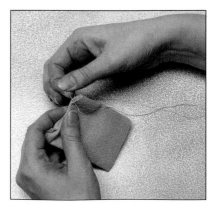

2 Turn both pieces right sides out and press. Slip stitch the open edge together.

3 Place the two pieces together with a slightly smaller piece of felt between. Stitch through all three layers by hand.

TIP

You can use any of the smaller motifs in this book to decorate needlecases, towels, tablecloths and table linen.

Pine cone card

Cross-stitch Christmas cards are always well received. This pine cone card suggests a winter countryside, but is refreshingly unlike traditional Christmas scenes.

YOU WILL NEED
Design size: 31 x 40
fabric: 14 hpi Aida, 10 x 10 cm
    (4 x 4 in)
26 tapestry needle
stranded cotton, as listed in key
iron
towel
card with opening
pencil
wadding (batting)
scissors
double-sided tape

1 Starting from the centre of the design, work the pine cone using two strands for cross stitch and one strand for backstitch.

2 When the work is complete, check it for marks. If it is grubby, you can rinse the stitching in warm, soapy water.

3 Allow it to dry flat and press lightly with the stitching face down on a towel so that you don't flatten the stitches.

4 Mount your work by following the instructions for filling a card.

card with opening

stranded cotton

26 tapestry needle

pencil

scissors

fabric

wadding (batting)

double-sided tape

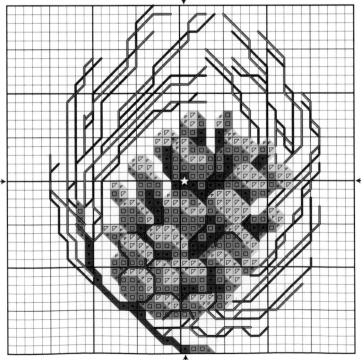

Cross stitch in two strands
- 391 Mushroom
- 393 Very dark brown
- 905 Mink brown

Backstitch in one strand
— 236 Dark grey
— 879 Very dark forest green
— 905 Mink brown

☆ Middle point

Holly and berries tree decoration

Cross-stitch tree decorations will make your Christmas tree stand out from the crowd this year. Why not set yourself a challenge and complete a whole set of decorations?

YOU WILL NEED
Design size: 37 x 36
fabric: 14 hpi Aida, 10 x 10 cm
   (4 x 4 in)
26 tapestry needle
stranded cotton, as listed in key
pencil
tape measure
scissors
sharp needle
sewing thread
8 cm (3 in) embroidery frame
felt

Cross stitch in two strands
1044 Dark grass green
246 Mid grass green
245 Privet green
47 Dark red
46 Berry red
307 Gold
298 Deep yellow

Backstitch in one strand
246 Mid grass green
47 Dark red
307 Gold

☆   Middle point

embroidery
frame

stranded
cotton

scissors

26 tapestry
needle

sewing
thread

needle

felt

pencil

fabric

tape measure

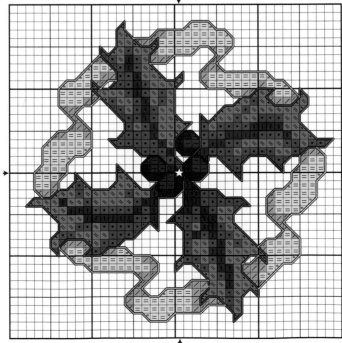

1 Work the design using two strands for cross stitch and one strand for backstitch. When complete, draw a 10 cm (4 in) circle around the design and cut it out.

2 Run a double gathering stitch 6 mm (¹/₄ in) inside the raw edge of the fabric. Position the design over the inside rim of the 8 cm (3 in) embroidery frame and draw up the gathering thread, ensuring that the design remains in the centre of the frame.

3 Lace the design into the back of the frame and replace the outside ring over the frame.

4 Finish by slip stitching a circle of felt over the back of your work.

Mistletoe bookmark

This bookmark is quick and easy to make. Placed inside a friend's favourite book, it will make a unique gift.

YOU WILL NEED
Design size: 26 x 110
fabric: 14 hpi Aida plus, 7.5 x 23 cm
  (3 x 9 in)
24 tapestry needle
stranded cotton, as listed in key
scissors
tape measure
sharp needle
sewing thread
ribbon

ribbon

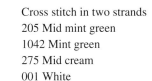
stranded cotton

scissors

24 tapestry needle

needle

fabric

sewing thread

tape measure

1 Work the design using two strands for cross stitch and one for backstitch. Cut around the finished design.

2 To make the tassel, cut seven lengths of light green Marlitt about 20 cm (8 in) long. Fold them in half to make a loop at the top.

3 Wrap a long thread around the threads just below the loop and stitch it through the threads. Stitch your tassel to the bottom of the bookmark.

4 To finish, slip stitch a piece of ribbon behind the bookmark. Trim to match the shape of the bookmark.

Cross stitch in two strands

□ □	205 Mid mint green
• •	1042 Mint green
⊠ ⊠	275 Mid cream
△ △	001 White

Backstitch in one strand

——	1042 Mint green
——	258 Dark mint green

☆   Middle point

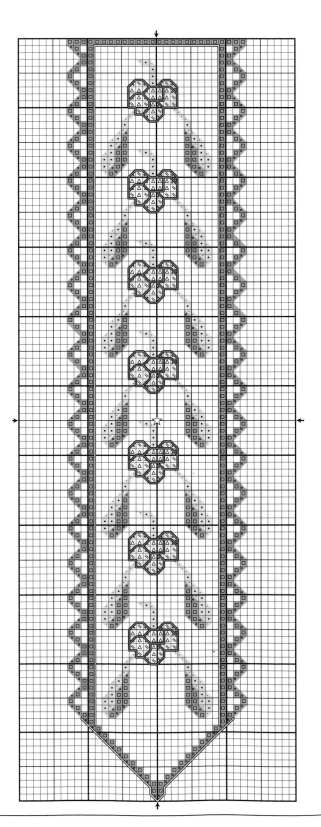

Snow scene birthday book

A birthday book is always a welcome gift. Make it appropriate for winter by filling it with a moody snow scene.

YOU WILL NEED
Design size: 45 x 57
fabric: 28 hpi evenweave over two
    threads, 15 x 20 cm (6 x 8 in)
26 tapestry needle
stranded cotton, as listed in key
iron
interfacing
pencil
scissors
craft birthday book
double-sided tape

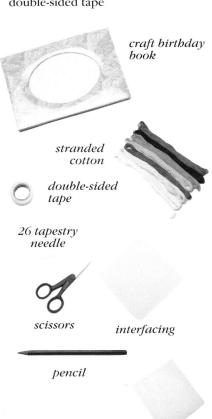

craft birthday book

stranded cotton

double-sided tape

26 tapestry needle

scissors

pencil

interfacing

fabric

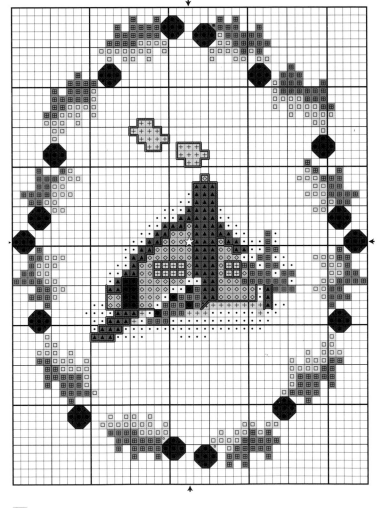

Cross stitch in two strands
860 Dark green
234 Light grey
367 Light brown
375 Dark brown
2 White
9046 Dark red
858 Light green

Backstitch in one strand
236 Dark grey

☆ Middle point

1 Work the design using two strands for cross stitch and one for backstitch.

2 Iron interfacing on to the back of the design.

3 Cut the fabric to fit the book.

4 Slide the design into the front pocket of the book and fix with double-sided tape.

TIP

When you start stitching avoid starting with a knot. If you are mounting your work against a flat surface, the knot will put pressure against the fabric and in time will weaken that area of material. Instead, bring your needle up through the fabric, leaving a tail at the back of your work. When making the first few stitches ensure you work them over the loose tail. These stitches will hold the thread firmly. To finish a length of thread, take it to the back of the work and thread the needle through the back of the last few stitches that were made. Cut the thread.

Holly bookmark

Deck the halls with holly or simply stitch some instead to create a border for this winter scene. This design will make a super present for a book lover.

YOU WILL NEED

Design size: 32 x 98
fabric: 18 hpi Aida bookmark,
  8 x 18 cm (3 x 7 in)
26 tapestry needle
stranded cotton, as listed in key
felt
ruler
fabric-marker pen
scissors
pins
sharp needle
sewing thread

bookmark

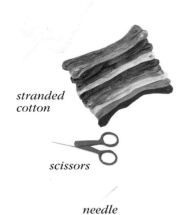

stranded cotton

scissors

needle

felt

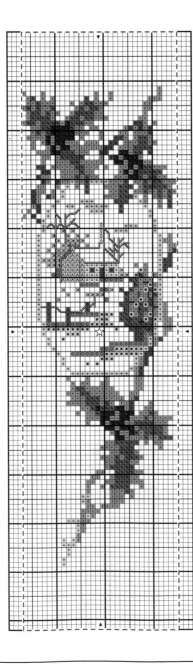

Cross stitch in two strands

• •	210 Grass green
∖ ∖	212 Dark green
▮ ▮	46 Berry red
– –	324 Dark orange
I I	374 Deep ochre
II II	359 Dark brown
+ +	9159 Pale blue
⊣•⊢ ⊣•⊢	890 Gold
÷ ÷	891 Light gold
∧ ∧	376 Very light beige
O O	8581 Grey
⊁ ⊁	848 Light blue grey
✳ ✳	231 Beige

Backstitch in one strand

——	46 Berry red
——	359 Dark brown
◦◦◦	848 Light grey blue

☆	Middle point

1 Work the cross stitch using two strands throughout.

2 Backstitch the detail, using one strand for each colour.

3 Neatly finish the work by following the instructions for making a bookmark.

Cottage snow scene card

A typical sight during the winter is the robin red-breast proudly singing his vibrant song. Perched on a branch, he cuts an imposing figure in the countryside.

YOU WILL NEED

Design size: 88 x 66
fabric: 18 hpi Aida, 17 x 17 cm
 (6½ x 6½ in)
26 tapestry needle
stranded cotton, as listed in key
card with opening
wadding (batting)
fabric-marker pen
scissors
double-sided tape

1 Work the cross stitch using two strands throughout.

2 Backstitch the detail on the chart using one strand for each colour.

3 Neatly finish your work and mount it by following the instructions for filling a card.

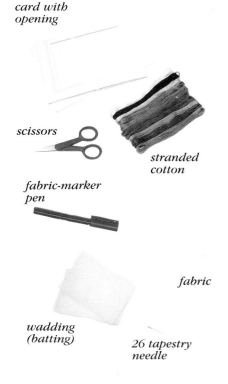

card with opening

scissors

stranded cotton

fabric-marker pen

fabric

wadding (batting)

26 tapestry needle

Cross stitch in two strands

■ ■	403 Black
+ +	1 White
✕ ✕	358 Dark mink
∧ ∧	375 Beige
И И	339 Salmon pink
＼ ＼	337 Pale salmon pink
／ ／	8581 Grey
◇ ◇	397 Pale grey
✕ ✕	212 Dark green
0 0	268 Dark hunter green
⊥ ⊥	280 Olive

Backstitch in one strand

— 403 Black

☆ Middle point

Garden fairy

Perched in a prime position on your tree, the garden fairy will bring a touch of country magic to your Christmas!

YOU WILL NEED

Design size: 70 x 74
fabric: 14 hpi plastic canvas,
  18 x 20 cm (7 x 8 in)
26 tapestry needle
stranded cotton, as listed in key
scissors
green felt, 18 x 20 cm (7 x 8 in)
sharp needle (optional)
sewing thread (optional)
gold thread

plastic canvas

gold thread

scissors

felt

needle

stranded cotton

Cross stitch in
three strands

II II	1 White
■■	19 Deep red
⠿	886 Beige
0 0	288 Pale yellow
● ●	291 Sunshine yellow
✱✱	926 Cream
◁◁	876 Mid blue green
▶▶	877 Mid sage green
↓↓	778 Pale pink
↑↑	4146 Mid blush

Backstitch in
one strand

—	879 Very dark blue green
—	19 Deep red
—◉	914 Dark pink

Backstitch in
two strands

—	Madeira no.40 gold 8

☆ Middle point

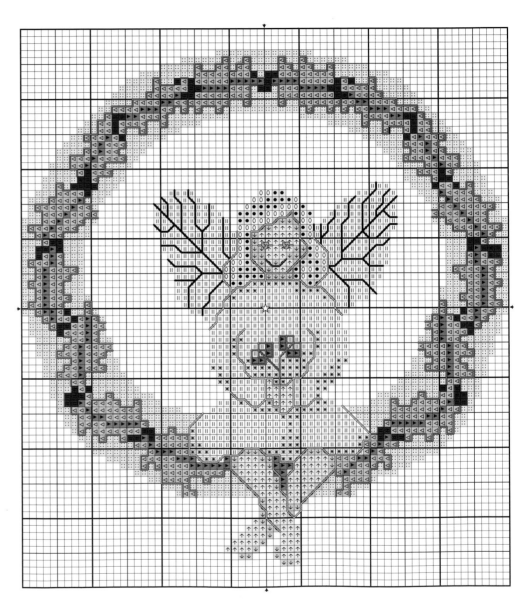

MAKING-UP INSTRUCTIONS

1 Work the cross stitch onto the plastic canvas using three strands throughout. Backstitch the detail, using one strand in the following colours: very dark blue green for holly wreath; deep red for mouth; dark pink for fairy. Use two strands of Madeira gold for backstitching on the wings. Stitch one French knot in dark pink for each fairy eye.

2 Carefully cut away the canvas around the edge of your design, taking care not to snip the stitches.

3 Oversew (slip stitch) the edges to cover all the raw canvas using two strands of very dark blue green.

4 Cut off any knobbly corners for a neat finish and attach the felt. You can either use sticky-backed felt or sew on ordinary felt using small invisible stitches.

Spider in web card

On cold, frosty mornings, when the sparkling frost transforms the leaves and grass, the spider's web gleams like diamonds.

YOU WILL NEED
Design size: 32 x 43
fabric: 14 hpi Aida, 10 x 15 cm
    (4 x 6 in)
26 tapestry needle
stranded cotton, as listed in key
iron
towel
card with opening
pencil
wadding (batting)
scissors
double-sided tape

1 Starting from the centre of the design, work the motif using two strands for cross stitch, two strands for backstitch on the legs and one strand for all remaining backstitch.

2 When the work is complete, check it for marks. If it is grubby, you can rinse the stitching in warm, soapy water.

3 Allow it to dry flat and press lightly with the stitching face down on a towel so that you don't flatten the stitches.

4 Mount your work by following the instructions for filling a card.

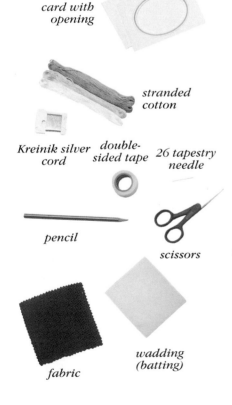

card with opening

stranded cotton

Kreinik silver cord

double-sided tape

26 tapestry needle

pencil

scissors

fabric

wadding (batting)

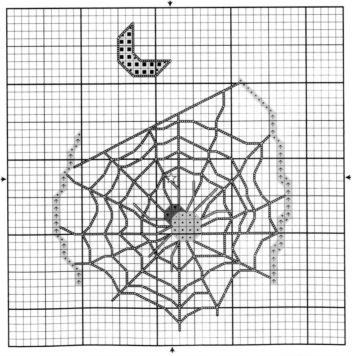

Cross stitch in two strands
234 Light grey
235 Dark grey
254 Dark yellow-green
386 Cream

Backstitch in two strands
234 Light grey

Backstitch in one strand
001C Kreinik silver cord

French knot in two strands
234 Light grey

☆ Middle point

Badger pot

Big and sturdy, slow and methodical, the badger is still quite a rare sight and certainly one to remember.

YOU WILL NEED
Design size: 37 x 33
fabric: 18 hpi Aida, 10 x 10 cm
   (4 x 4 in)
26 tapestry needle
stranded cotton, as listed in key
iron
towel
7 cm (2½ in) craft pot
pencil
scissors
wadding (batting)

stranded cotton

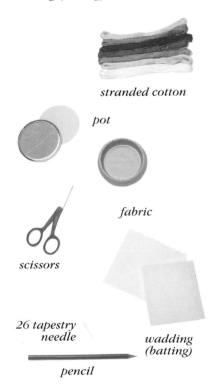

pot

fabric

scissors

26 tapestry needle

wadding (batting)

pencil

1 Starting from the centre of the design, work the motif using two strands for cross stitch and dark green backstitch, and one strand for French knots and remaining backstitch.

2 When the work is complete, check it for marks. If it is grubby, you can rinse the stitching in warm, soapy water.

3 Allow it to dry flat and press lightly with the stitching face down on a towel so that you don't flatten the stitches.

4 Mount your work by following the instructions for filling a pot.

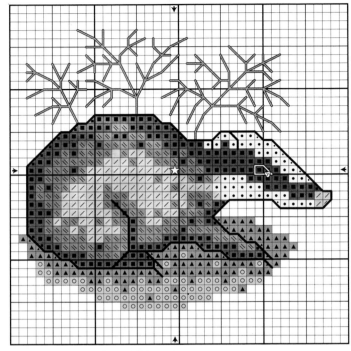

Cross stitch in two strands
236 Dark grey
399 Light grey
842 Light green
843 Dark green
2 White
235 Mid grey

Backstitch in one strand
403 Black
2 White

Backstitch in two strands
843 Dark green

French knot in one strand
2 White

☆ Middle point

Mice clock

In "Hickory Dickory Dock" the mouse ran up the clock. In this design, cute mice run around the clock. This is an ideal beginner's project.

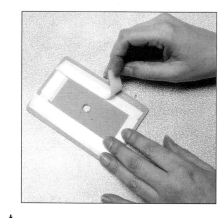

YOU WILL NEED
Design size: 58 x 84
fabric: 18 hpi Aida, 15 x 13 cm
   (6 x 5 in)
26 tapestry needle
stranded cotton, as listed in key
double-sided tape
small craft clock

MAKING-UP INSTRUCTIONS

1 Work the design using two strands for cross stitch and French knots, and one strand for backstitch. Attach double-sided tape around the edges of the piece of cardboard supplied with the clock.

2 Place the design face down on a flat surface and place the cardboard on top with the double-sided tape uppermost. Stick the edges on to the cardboard.

small clock

stranded cotton

fabric

26 tapestry needle

double-sided tape

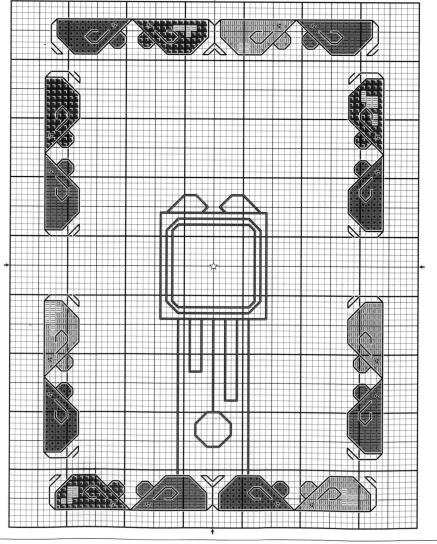

Cross stitch in two strands

936 Mid brown
1041 Dark grey
1046 Mid reddish-brown
234 Pearl grey
387 Mid cream

Backstitch in one strand

403 Black
905 Mink brown

French knot in two strands

403 Black

☆ Middle point

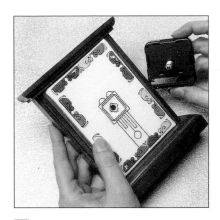

 Place the design in the clock frame facing outwards. Fix the clock movement into the back of the clock.

4 To finish, attach the hands.

TIP

You can use double-sided tape to fix your work to the back of a board before framing. It is satisfactory as a temporary measure, or on something you don't expect to last. For a more permanent method, follow the instructions for lacing a picture.

Mistletoe gift tag

When you give your Christmas presents surprise the recipients with dainty, hand-stitched tags.

YOU WILL NEED
Design size: 18 x 19
fabric: 18 hpi Aida, 9 x 8 cm
  (3½ x 3 in)
stranded cotton, as listed in key
26 tapestry needle
3 pearl beads
gift tag with opening
wadding (batting)
fabric-marker pen
scissors
double-sided tape

1 Work the cross stitch using one strand throughout.

2 Backstitch the detail, using one strand for each colour.

3 Neatly finish off the work and mount in a gift tag by following the instructions for filling a card.

gift tag with opening   *fabric*

wadding (batting)   *stranded cotton*

scissors

fabric-marker pen

26 tapestry needle

Cross stitch in one strand
- 243 Mid green
- 264 Yellow green
- 292 Light lemon
- Pearl bead

Backstitch in one strand
— 243 Mid green
— 264 Yellow green

☆ Middle point

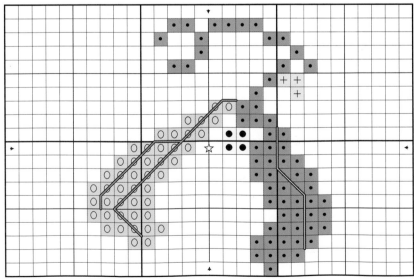

Cyclamen card

This is not much evidence of flowers during the winter months, yet in households across the land the cyclamen blooms eternal.

YOU WILL NEED
Design size: 29 x 44
fabric: 18 hpi Aida, 10 x 13 cm
  (4 x 5 in)
26 tapestry needle
stranded cotton, as listed in key
card with opening
wadding (batting)
fabric-marker pen
scissors
double-sided tape

1 Work the cross stitch using two strands throughout.

2 Backstitch the detail, using one strand for each colour.

3 Neatly finish your work and mount it by following the instructions for filling a card.

card with opening

stranded cotton

scissors

wadding (batting)

fabric-marker pen

fabric

26 tapestry needle

Cross stitch in two strands

∧∧	876 Mid blue green
ИИ	875 Light blue green
◥◥	878 Dark blue green
⁄⁄	63 Mid cranberry
⊃⊃	55 Mid pink
■	78 Dark cranberry

Backstitch in one strand

— 69 Mauve

— 879 Very dark blue green

☆ Middle point

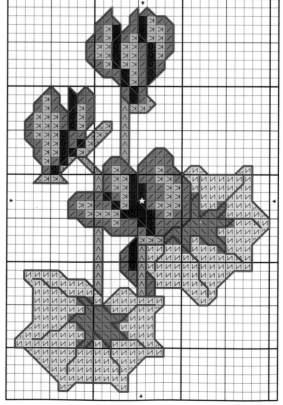

Winter cushion

With holly, mistletoe and Christmas roses, this elegant cushion will make an elegant centrepiece for your festive display.

YOU WILL NEED
Design size: 133 x 142
fabric: 14 hpi navy blue Aida,
  36 x 36 cm (14 x 14 in)
26 tapestry needle
thimble
stranded cotton, as listed in key
backing fabric
tape measure
fabric-marker pen
scissors
pins
sharp needle
sewing thread
cushion pad

backing fabric

tape measure

stranded cotton

sewing thread

pins

thimble

scissors

needle

Cross stitch in two strands

⌶⌶	1 White
+ +	1/213 White/very light leaf green
⌧⌧	1/875 White/light blue green
⋉⋉	289/288 Yellow/pale yellow
∧∧	238 Bright green
И И	238/288 Bright green/pale yellow
◢	13 Christmas red
◥	19 Deep red
⊳⊳	265 Light green
═ ═	268 Dark hunter green
□ □	266 Light hunter green
↓↓	393 Very dark mushroom
⊥⊥	288 Pale yellow
← ←	393/903 Very dark mushroom/dark mocha
△ △	898 Mid brown
⋉⋉	289/888 Yellow/deep mocha
→ →	246 Deep pine green
↑↑	244 Mid pine green
■ ■	243 Light green
● ●	46 Berry red
▲ ▲	778 Pale pink
⌶⌶	289 Yellow

Backstitch in one strand

——	860 Slate green
══	1 White
····	936 Dark brown
——	19 Deep red
····	924 Deep olive green
····	246 Deep pine

Backstitch and French knots in two strands

◠	288 Pale yellow
◔	289 Yellow
☆	Middle point

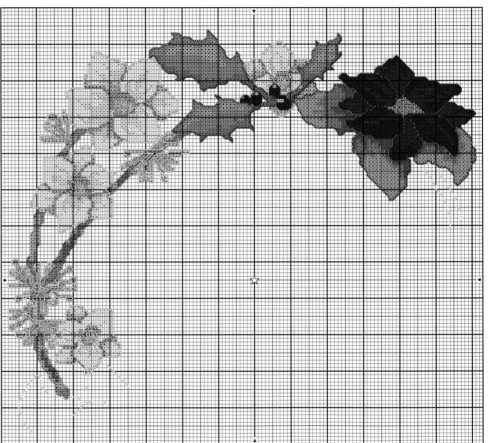

1 Work the cross stitch using two strands throughout.

2 Backstitch the detail, using one strand, for each of the following colours: slate green for lines dividing the Christmas rose petals; white for outside edges of Christmas roses; dark brown dividing poinsettia petals; deep red for outside edges of poinsettia flowers; deep olive green for outlines of poinsettia leaves; deep pine green for holly leaves. Use two strands for long stitch in pale yellow for stamens of Christmas rose, and two strands for French knots: pale yellow at the end of each Christmas rose stamen and yellow randomly to fill the centre of the poinsettia flowers.

3 Finish off the work and make into a cushion, following the instructions for the Spring cushion.

Pansy picture

Berlin wool work was one of the most popular pastimes in Victorian England. The designs, which were usually preprinted, featured favourite pets, birds and flowers. This pretty pansy is reminiscent of the traditional style and is easily worked following the cross-stitch chart.

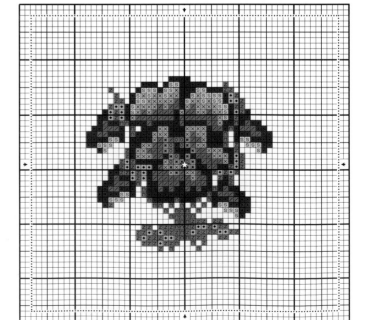

YOU WILL NEED
Design size: 56 x 54
fabric: 10 hpi antique double-thread
  canvas, 23 x 23 cm (9 x 9 in)
sharp needle
tacking (basting) thread
pins
embroidery frame
tapestry needle
tapestry wool, as listed in key

1 Tack (baste) guide lines along the centre of the canvas in both directions. Pin the canvas onto the embroidery frame.

2 Work the design in half cross stitch from the bottom of the motif to the top.

3 Count out 12 squares from each side of the pansy and tack (baste) a guide line to mark the edge of the background. Begin at the bottom and work rows in one direction only, filling in around the pansy as required. Use fairly short lengths of wool and sew ends back into the worked stitches before trimming.

4 Neatly finish the work and mount it by following the instructions for lacing a frame.

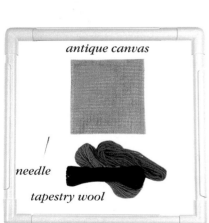

antique canvas

needle

tapestry wool

embroidery frame

Cross stitch in one strand

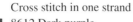

Symbol	Colour
◼◼	8612 Dark purple
╱╱	8608 Purple
✕✕	8602 Light purple
SS	8584 Pale purple
✳✳	8024 Gold
OO	9510 Pink
⌐⌐	9216 Moss green
ZZ	9308 Heraldic gold
◆◆	9290 Olive

☆ Middle point

Wave glasses case

This elegant wave-inspired spectacle case would make an ideal gift for a friend or relative. You could make it in their favourite colour scheme.

YOU WILL NEED
fabric: 26 hpi black evenweave,
   20 x 20 cm (8 x 8 in)
ruler
sharp needle
tacking (basting) thread
embroidery frame
26 tapestry needle
stranded cotton, as listed in key
scissors
black silk cord, 40 cm (16 in)
black cotton fabric, 20 x 20 cm
   (8 x 8 in)

cotton fabric

scissors

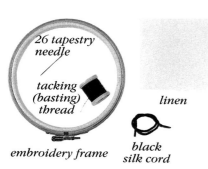

stranded cotton

26 tapestry needle

tacking (basting) thread

linen

embroidery frame

black silk cord

1 On the linen mark out a 16 cm (6¼ in) square with tacking (basting) thread and fit the material into a large embroidery frame.

2 Beginning 2.5 cm (1 in) up from the tacking (basting) line, work a band of Florentine stitch across the linen. Each stitch is worked in six strands of cotton. Work vertical stitches over six threads of the linen. Begin the next step three threads up or down, but make it the same length. Grade the colours and vary the width of steps to create a band of embroidery 8 cm (3 in) wide.

3 Trim the seam allowances to 2.5 cm (1 in) and press on the wrong side with a damp cloth. Fold the material in half with right sides together. Using the new seam allowances throughout, stitch down the side and along the bottom of the case. Trim the seams and corners. Turn the material through and fold down a 2.5 cm (1 in) hem along the top. Slip stitch silk cord around the top and down the seam, sewing the ends securely on the inside. Make a lining the same shape from black cotton fabric. Tuck the lining inside the spectacle case and slip stitch around the top edge.

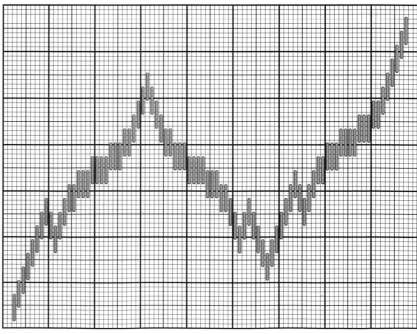

Vertical stitches in six strands
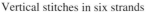
145 Blue
343 Very pale blue
875 Very pale green
877 Light blue green
851 Dark turquoise

Christmas bows

These beautiful bows have many uses. As well as decorating the tree, they could be used to hold up a swathe of holly and ivy above the hearth. Fixed to curtain tiebacks they will add a simple, but effective, festive touch.

YOU WILL NEED
Design size: 82 x 40
fabric: red and white evenweave
  bonds, 5 x 71 cm (2 x 28 in)
sharp needle
tacking (basting) thread
ruler
pencil
26 tapestry needle
stranded cotton, as shown in key
brass florist's wire (floral wire),
  10 cm (4 in)

linen

sewing thread

evenweave band

tacking (basting) thread

Kreinik cable *florist's wire*

stranded cotton *needle*

ruler

1 Fold the evenweave band in half widthways and mark the centre line with tacking (basting) stitches. Measure and mark 3 cm (1¼ in) and 9 cm (3½ in) either side of the centre. Within these areas, count the threads and mark the horizontal and vertical centre lines.

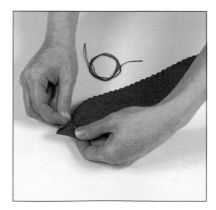

2 Tack (baste) guide lines for the cross stitch. The centre should be 6 cm (2¼ in) from the end of the fabric. Turn the ends of the bows in 1 cm (½ in) and mitre the corners.

3 Following the chart, stitch the design at either end of the fabric on the right side using two strands of cotton over two threads of the evenweave. Turn the fabric over and stitch the design for the centre of the bow on the reverse side. Fold the fabric in three using the 9 cm (3½ in) marks as a guide for the width. Sew long running stitches down the centre mark to sew all layers of the fabric together. Use six strands of matching stranded cotton. Gather the fabric and wrap the thread round five times. Stitch to secure.

4 Remove the tacking (basting) stitches and sew the wire to the back of the bow.

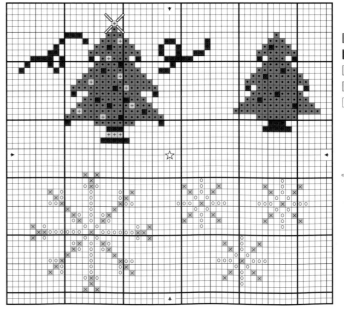

Cross stitch
in two strands

••	230 Green
▦	47 Red
++	Gold Kreinik
××	Silver Kreinik
○○	1 White

Half cross stitch
in one strand
radiating from
centre
— Gold Kreinik

☆ Middle point

Poinsettia ornaments

Brighten up your Christmas tree with these imaginative, easy-to-stitch ornaments.

YOU WILL NEED
Design size: 24 x 19
fabric: 18 hpi Aida, 12 x
  12 cm (4¾ x 4¾ in)
26 tapestry needle
stranded cotton, as listed in key
fabric-marker pen
scissors
sharp needle
sewing thread
polystyrene ball
gold braid
ribbon or tassel
glue
felt

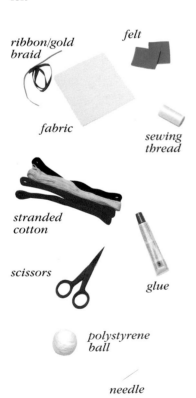

ribbon/gold braid   *felt*

fabric   *sewing thread*

stranded cotton   *glue*

scissors

polystyrene ball

needle

MAKING-UP INSTRUCTIONS

1 Work the cross stitch using two strands throughout. Backstitch around the outline, using one strand of black. Once the design has been worked, cut a circle from the fabric with the design in the centre. Run a gathering thread around the edge of the circle and pull it up around the polystyrene ball.

2 Attach a loop of braid to the top of the ball to make a hanging hook.

3 Tie a bow from ribbon at the base of the braid or sew on a tassel.

4 Finish by gluing a small circle of felt over the gathering at the back.

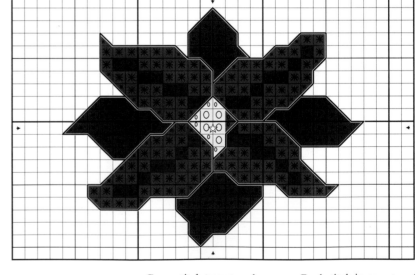

Cross stitch two strands	Backstitch in one strand
19 Deep red	— 403 Black
13 Christmas red	
289 Yellow	☆ Middle point

Advent calendar

With 24 days to Christmas Eve, you can mark each one by stitching this advent calendar, complete with brass rings, on which you can hang candies to note each day of the countdown.

1 Work the cross stitch using two strands throughout. Backstitch the stamens of flowers in two strands of sunshine yellow and two strands of mid hunter green for the oval surround. Stitch French knots in sunshine yellow at the end of each stamen. Backstitch the remaining detail using one strand for each of the following colours: mid hunter green for the leaves and stems; very dark flesh for the flowers.

2 Wash and iron the work prior to adding the curtain rings. Attach each curtain ring using two strands of mid hunter green and making two cross stitches over two threads of even-weave. Insert the needle from the back of the fabric and through the curtain ring. Take the needle down though the appropriate hole to make the lower half of the first cross stitch and pass it through the loop on the back. Pull to your normal tension. Complete two full cross stitches and cast off firmly.

YOU WILL NEED

Design size: 54 x 84 (central panel)
fabric: 28 hpi evenweave over
 two threads, 24 x 26 cm
 (9½ x 10¼ in)
26 tapestry needles
thimble
stranded cotton, as listed in key
iron
24 small brass curtain rings
picture frame
cardboard
tape measure
fabric-marker pen
scissors
wadding (batting)
pins
sharp needle
sewing thread
5m (180 in) reel of 5 mm
 (¼ in) green silk ribbon
24 wrapped candies

curtain rings

stranded cotton

scissors

fabric

candies

fabric-marker pen

thimble

tape measure

sewing thread

pins

needle

ribbon

Cross stitch in
two strands

▽▽	1 White
◩◪	267 Mid hunter green
＼＼	288 Pale yellow
ͶͶ	291 Sunshine yellow
∧∧	926 Off white
●●	262 Olive green
７７	259 Very light green

For backstitch
and French
knot details
see Step 1

—🖉 291 Sunshine yellow

—— 267 Mid hunter green

—— 914 Very dark flesh

☆ Middle point

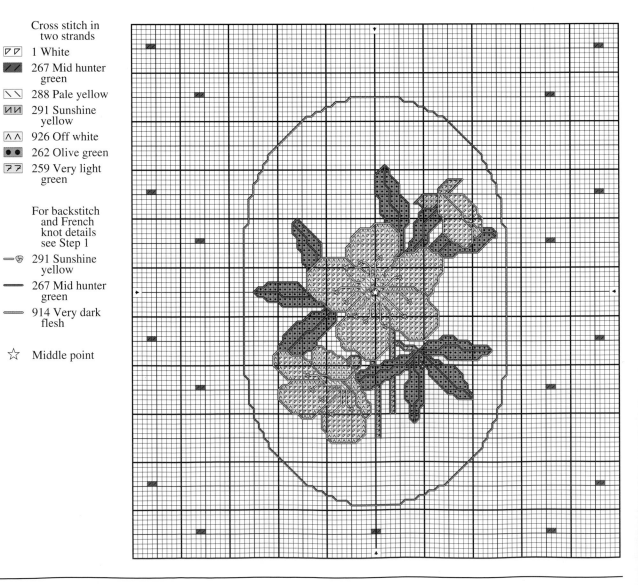

MAKING-UP INSTRUCTIONS

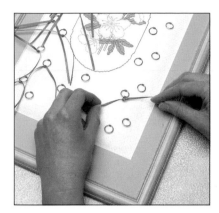

1 Mount the work following the instructions for lacing a frame. Cut 24 pieces of ribbon 20 cm (8 in) in length, and tie them to the brass rings.

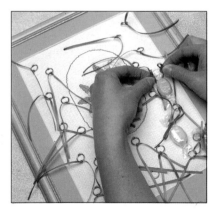

2 Tie a wrapped candy into the ribbon by first placing the candy onto the knot and then tying a bow over it.

Winter cottage

Winter may seem bleak, but don't despair. Look around at the distinctive colours of the season. This cottage brings together all the glorious tones and hues that denote winter.

YOU WILL NEED
Design size: 106 x 76
fabric: 30 hpi linen over two
   threads, 26 x 20 cm (10¼ x 8 in)
26 tapestry needle
stranded cotton, as listed in key
picture frame
cardboard
tape measure
fabric-marker pen
scissors
wadding (batting)
pins
sharp needle
sewing thread

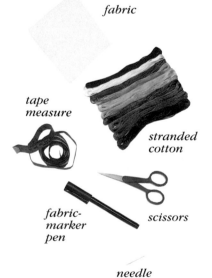

fabric

tape measure

stranded cotton

fabric-marker pen

scissors

needle

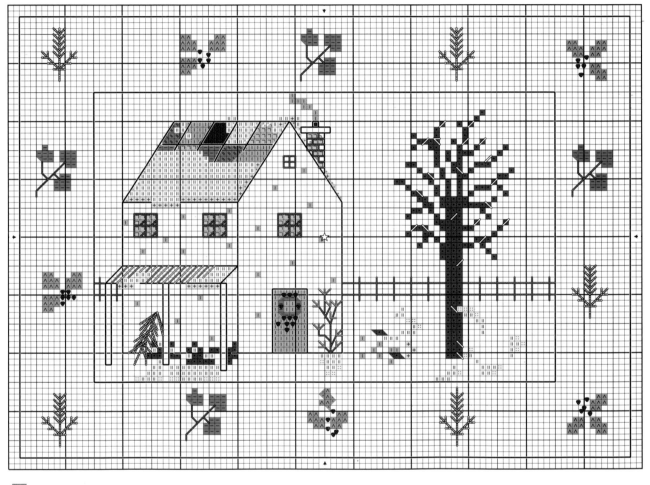

1 Work the cross stitch in two strands throughout.

2 Backstitch the outline and details using one strand for each colour. Use deep pink French knots for holly berries, Christmas garland and door knob.

3 Neatly finish off your work and mount it by following the instructions for lacing a frame.

Cross stitch in two strands

∧∧ 227 Light green
●●● 360 Brown
╲╲ 169 Mid turquoise
⌐⌐ 868 Candy pink
━━ 923 Deep Christmas green
Ⅰ Ⅰ 903 Dark mocha
Ⅱ Ⅱ 1 White
+ + 976 Pastel blue

∧∧ 227 Light green
0 0 1029 Deep pink
∷∷ 976/1 Pastel blue/ white

Backstitch in one strand
——— 360 Brown
········· 227/903 Light green/ dark mocha
——— 403 Black

——— 169 Mid turquoise
——— 903 Dark mocha
——— 227 Light green
══ 976/1 Bright leaf green/white

French knots in one strand
♥ 1029 Deep pink
☆ Middle point

Robin Christmas stocking

Imagine Santa coming to your home and finding this charming stocking. He'll be sure to fill it full of wonderful treats.

YOU WILL NEED

Design size: 53 x 62
fabric: 28 hpi evenweave over
 two threads, 36 x 25 cm
 (14 x 10 in)
26 tapestry needle
stranded cotton, as listed in key
36 cm (14 in) of backing fabric
tape measure
fabric marker pen
scissors
lightweight iron-on interfacing
iron
sharp needle
sewing thread
20 cm (8 in) ribbon

Cross stitch in
two strands

⠂⠂	1 White
‖ ‖	11 Red coral
■■	19 Deep red
✳✳	362 Pale apricot
⊥⊥	877 Blue grass green
＼＼	403 Black
／／	234 Light slate grey
∧∧	901 Mahogany
⑈⑈	277 Mid mink

Backstitch in
one strand

— 879 Very dark blue green
— 72 Deep wine
— 905 Brown

French knots in
one strand

♋ 1 White

☆ Middle point

fabric

iron-on interfacing

backing fabric

stranded cotton

ribbon

scissors

sewing thread

needle

tape measure

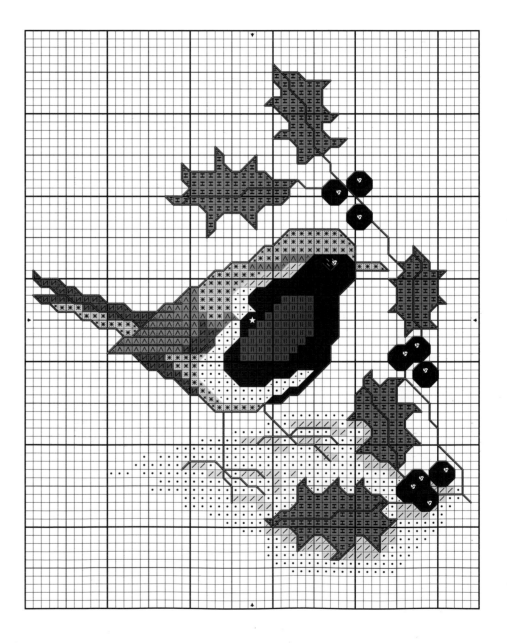

MAKING-UP INSTRUCTIONS

1 Cut out three stocking shapes, one from the evenweave and a pair in backing fabric. Position the design in the centre of the evenweave fabric and work the cross stitch using two strands throughout. Backstitch the detail, using one strand, in the following colours: very dark blue green for the leaves and stems; deep wine for berries and red breast; brown for the rest of the robin. Use one strand of white for French knots for the eye and on the berries. When the design is complete, iron on lightweight interfacing to the wrong side of the evenweave to reduce fraying.

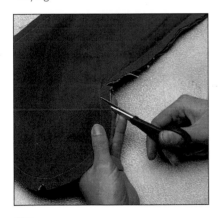

2 Place the evenweave and backing fabric stocking pieces right sides together and stitch around the boot and up the sides of the stocking, leaving the top edge open. At the top turn over a 1.5 cm (⅝ in) hem and stitch around the hem. Turn and press.

SEWING TIP
Never iron directly on to your cross stitch. Always use a dampened cloth over the design to preserve your work.

3 Place remaining backing fabric stocking right side to embroidered surface of evenweave. Top edge will be approximately 1.5 cm (⅝ in) above the finished top edge of the front. Stitch around the stocking. Clip curves. Turn right side out and press.

4 Fold a top seam allowance 1.5 cm (⅝ in) inside stocking and hem, enclosing the hanging ribbon at the back seam.

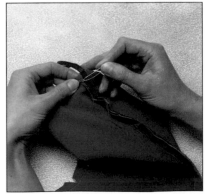

Christmas tree decoration

A simple flexihoop makes a super Christmas tree decoration. Stitch this tree to hang on yours. It's a project which can be attempted by the novice stitcher.

YOU WILL NEED
Design size: 25 x 32
fabric: 28 hpi evenweave over
   two threads, 12 x 13 cm
   (4¾ x 5 in)
26 tapestry needle
stranded cotton, as listed in key
embroidery frame 6 x 9 cm
   (2¼ x 3½ in)
ruler
fabric marker pen
scissors
sharp needle
sewing thread
felt for backing, 12 x 13 cm
   (4¾ x 5 in)

1 Work the cross stitch using two strands throughout.

2 Finish the work neatly and place the design in the embroidery frame. Cut the fabric to within one inch of the hoop and sew running stitches around the edge. Pull up the gathers and lace across the back. Cut the felt to the same size and slip stitch to the fabric with invisible stitches. Replace the outside ring.

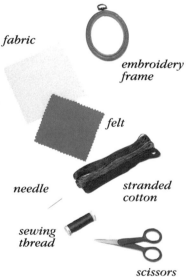

fabric

embroidery frame

felt

needle

stranded cotton

sewing thread

scissors

Cross stitch in two strands
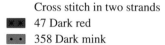
✶✶ 47 Dark red
• • 358 Dark mink
○ ○ 244 Mid pine green

☆ Middle point

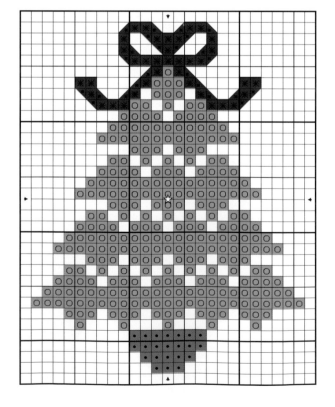

Bird table

It's not easy for birds in winter. The pickings are poor. Some kind people make their lives more pleasurable by stretching out the hand of generosity and leaving them titbits.

YOU WILL NEED
Design size: 51 x 67
fabric: 14 hpi Aida, 17 x 18 cm
  (6½ x 7 in)
26 tapestry needle
stranded cotton, as listed in key
picture frame
cardboard
tape measure
fabric marker pen
scissors
wadding (batting)
pins
sharp needle
sewing thread

1 Work the cross stitch using two strands throughout. Use two strands of very light brown for back stitching on branches and lemon for back stitching blackbird's legs and beak.

2 Backstitch remaining detail using one strand for each colour. Use two strands for French knots in yellow for blackbird's eye and black for others.

3 Neatly finish off your work, and mount it by following the instructions for lacing a frame.

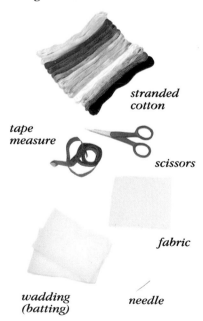

stranded cotton

tape measure

scissors

fabric

wadding (batting)

needle

Cross stitch in two strands

O O	351 Mid mink
□ □	288 Very pale yellow
↓ ↓	398 Pearl grey
⊓ ⊓	403 Black
I I	9046 Dark red
– –	4146 Light peach flesh
+ +	362 Pale apricot
÷ ÷	289 Yellow
к к	901 Very light brown
∧ ∧	167 Turquoise
и и	886 Beige
⋊ ⋊	1 White
• •	235 Steel grey

For backstitch and French knot details see Steps 1 and 2

═══	901 Very light brown
═☞	289 Yellow
═══	235 Steel grey
═══	9046 Dark red
═☞	403 Black
═══	360 Mid brown
☆	Middle point

Winter sampler

Mark the occasion by stitching this traditional sampler and make it a Christmas worth remembering.

1 Work the cross stitch using two strands throughout.

2 Backstitch the detail, using one strand for each colour. Use three strands for backstitching the robin's legs. Stitch a French knot in chocolate brown for the door handle.

3 Neatly finish the work. and mount it by following the instructions for lacing a frame.

YOU WILL NEED
Design size: 108 x 148
fabric: 28 hpi evenweave over
  two threads, 29 x 36 cm
  (11½ x 14 in)
26 tapestry needle
stranded cotton, as listed in key
picture frame
cardboard
tape measure
fabric-marker pen
scissors
wadding (batting)
pins
sharp needle
sewing thread

fabric-marker pen

scissors

fabric

needle

wadding

sewing thread

stranded cotton

Cross stitch in
  two strands

∙∙	332 Red
◥◥	326 Rusty orange
⌐⌐	1 White
--	399 Mid grey
⊏⊐	360 Mid brown
II II	926 Cream
++	379 Mink brown
✕✕	234/975 Pale grey/ pale blue
KK	277 Sienna brown
∧∧	267 Mid olive green
⊳⊲	268 Deep hunter green
■	13 Christmas red
○○	6 Salmon pink
□□	831 Dark beige
↓↓	392 Dark beige grey
←←	382 Chocolate brown
⬉⬉	393 Very dark mushroom
↑↑	976 Lilac
■■	868 Mid salmon
⌶⌶	9575 Deep salmon

Backstitch and French
  knots in one strand.
  Use three strands for
  backstitching robin's
  legs.

━●	382 Chocolate brown
━━	9575 Deep salmon
┄┄	360 Brown
━━	379 Mink brown
══	399 Mid grey
☆	Middle point

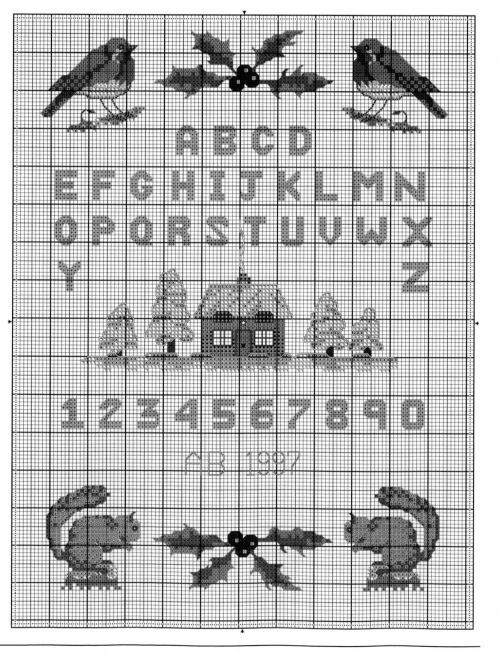

Butterfly brooch

Typically Victorian, this butterfly would look most elegant on a simple black dress. It could also be pinned to a belt or even used as a hair ornament for a special occasion.

YOU WILL NEED

fabric: close-woven black cotton,
 20 x 20 cm (8 x 8 in)
tracing paper
pencil
embroidery frame
sharp needle
black sewing thread
large round, iridescent beads
large and small long black beads
scissors
ruler
black felt, 20 x 20 cm (8 x 8 in)
cardboard
double-sided tape
fabric glue
brooch pin

1 Trace the butterfly design and transfer on to black fabric. Fit the material into an embroidery frame.

2 Sew the large round, iridescent beads individually to make the eyes and highlights of the wings. Use a double thread and begin with a knot. Outline the butterfly with small long beads and fill in the background with small round beads.

3 Cut out the butterfly leaving a 5 mm (¼ in) border all round. Remember to snip into the curves. Cut the shape of the butterfly from felt and cardboard. Score down each side of the "body" on the cardboard butterfly and turn over. Cut bits of double-sided tape to fit round the edge. Stretch the beaded fabric onto the cardboard shape.

4 Glue the felt shape on to the back of the brooch. Allow to dry before sewing the bead feelers on to the head and the brooch pin on to the back. Gently bend the wings forward.

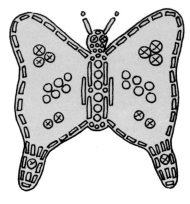

Fill in background with small beads.

⊗ ~ black iridescent beads, all others in plain black.

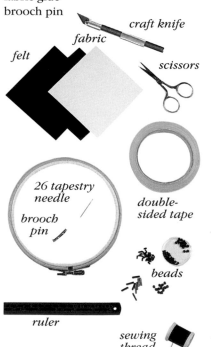

felt

fabric

craft knife

scissors

26 tapestry needle

brooch pin

double-sided tape

beads

ruler

sewing thread

Christmas tassel

Tassels were very popular in Victorian times for embellishing all manner of things. The Rocaile beads for this beautiful tassel came from an old necklace, but modern equivalents are readily available and may be used instead.

YOU WILL NEED
beading needle
Rocaile size 8 beads
ruler
Kreinik silver cord, 30 cm (12 in)
sharp needle
sewing cotton (thread)
white felt, 20 x 1.5 cm (8 x 5/8 in)
silver cord, 15 cm (6 in)
scissors
fabric glue
silver lurex yarn

1 Using the beading needle, thread beads on to the Kreinik silver cord until the beads measure 9 cm (3½ in). Miss the last bead and take the needle and cord back through all the other beads. Make about 38 strings of beads and stitch securely at 5 mm (¼ in) intervals to the strip of felt. Ensure each string is the same length. Taper the end of the felt to a point.

2 Fold the thick silver cord in half and tie a knot to form a loop. Sew the loop to the wide end of the felt, spread glue along the centre and roll up tightly. Stitch to secure. Wrap some lurex yarn round the felt ball to create a neat head.

3 Using Kreinik silver cord, sew strings of beads over the head from top to bottom. Stitch through the felt, continuing to add rows of beads until it is completely covered. Finish off the silver cord securely. Alternatively, the head of the tassel may be covered in detached buttonhole stitch.

fabric glue

sewing cotton

lurex yarn

Rocaile beads

cord

dressmaker's scissors

felt

embroidery scissors

Kreinik cord

beading needle   *sharp needle*

ruler

TIP
The head of the tassel can be covered in silky thread using detached buttonhole stitch instead of beads.

ACKNOWLEDGEMENTS

Publishers' Acknowledgements
The Publishers are grateful to the following companies who supplied materials used for photography:

Coats Crafts UK
PO Box 22, The Lingfield Estate, McMullen Road, Darlington, County Durham, DL1 1YQ, 01325 394 394. *Suppliers of Anchor embroidery threads.*

Fabric Flair
The Old Brewery, The Close, Warminster, Wiltshire, BA12 9AL. Tel: 01985 846845. *Suppliers.*

Framecraft Miniatures Limited
372/376 Summer Lane, Hockley, Birmingham, B19 3QA. Tel: 0121 212 0551. *Mail order suppliers of miniatures and cards.*

Contributors
The Publishers are grateful to the following contributors whose work appears in this book:
Alison Burton: Apple and pear placemats; Dragonfly card; Hedgehog pot; Holly and berries tree decoration; Nightgown case; Otter pot; Pears table set; Pine cone card; Poinsettia ornaments; Rabbit coaster; Spring sampler; Squirrel paperweight; Winter cushion; Winter sampler.
Christine Coggans: Aconites sampler (design).
Sara Creasy: Bees and honey tea towel; Christmas tree decoration; Garden card; Halloween pumpkin.
Lucinda Ganderton: Napkin and napkin ring.
Lesley Grant: Autumn cushion; Autumn scene; Bees padded coat hanger; Butterfly gift tags; Deer and fawn picture; Fledglings picture; Holly bookmark; Kingfisher shopping bag; Love cushion; Spring cushion; Summer garland; Summer meadow picture.
Kate Hanson-Smith: Pansy picture.
Alison Harper: Wave spectacle case.
Rachel Hyde: Chicken tea cosy; Collector's roses; Cottage snow scene picture; Lavender bag; Summer cushion.
Maureen Kennaugh: Butterfly shoulder-bag; Honeysuckle café curtain border design; Peacock book cover.
Evelyn King: Mistletoe gift tag; Summer roses hat band.
Brenda Monk: Alphabet sampler.
Dawn Parmley: Owl apron; Swan purse.
Penelope Randall: Corn-cob pot; Doves in cote card; Frogs on waterlilies tray cloth.
Jane Rimmer: Daisy shelf border; Duckling school gym bag.
Carolyn Sibbald: Christmas bows; Christmas tassel.
Barbara Smith: Lavender hat band; Mice clock.
Zoë Smith: Bluebells cushion; Buttercup cushion; Primrose picture frame.
Julia Tidmarsh: Aconites sampler (stitching); Advent calendar; Apple-blossom coffee pot cover; Autumn leaves pot stand; Baby fawn; Badger pot; Bird in bath; Bird table; Blackberry card; Blossom tree; Country flowers scissors case; Cyclamen card; Cyclamen footstool cover; First snowdrops; Fox pot; Foxglove mirror back; Garden fairy; Golden pheasant cabinet; Harvest mouse; Ladybird paperweight; Lilac print; Nesting squirrel pot; Oak tree hanging; Pig pot; Poppy doorplate; Posy of pansies; Rainbow bookmark; Robin Christmas stocking; Robin needlecase; Snow scene birthday book; Spider in web card; Strawberry paperweight; Summer house; Swallows pot; Trout print; Violet glasses case.
Lynda Whittle: Heron card; Mistletoe bookmark; Mushrooms in basket card; Wild rose card.
Dorothy Wood: Butterfly brooch; Coasters and table mat; Lavender needlecase. Thanks also to Dorothy Wood as author of the projects taken from *50 Step-by-Step Victorian Needlecraft Designs.*

Photographers
Most of the photographs in this book were taken by **Amanda Heywood**. The Publishers are also grateful to **Karl Adamson** for taking photographs for the following projects: Alphabet sampler; Butterfly brooch; Christmas bows; Christmas tassel; Coaster and table mat; Napkin and napkin ring; Lavender needlecase; Pansy picture; Wave spectacle case.